Medicine:
A MATTER OF LIFE AND DEATH

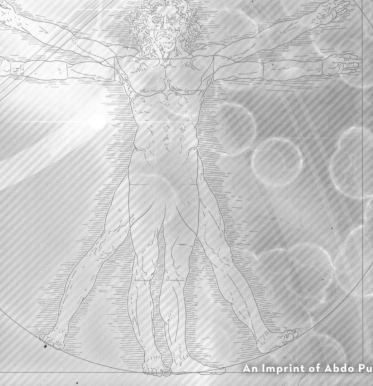

Essential Library

An Imprint of Abdo Publishing | www.abdopublishing.com

History *of* Science

Medicine:
A MATTER OF LIFE AND DEATH

by Russell Roberts

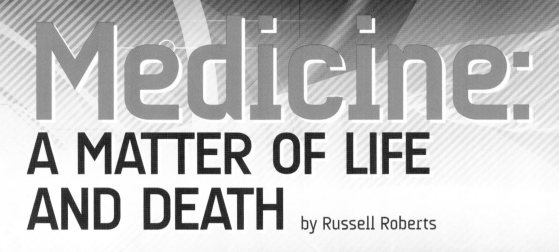

Content Consultant

Kristen Ann Ehrenberger, PhD
MD Candidate (2016), Medical Scholars Program
University of Illinois at Urbana-Champaign

History of Science

www.**abdopublishing.com**

Published by Abdo Publishing, a division of ABDO, PO Box 398166, Minneapolis, Minnesota 55439. Copyright © 2015 by Abdo Consulting Group, Inc. International copyrights reserved in all countries. No part of this book may be reproduced in any form without written permission from the publisher. Essential Library™ is a trademark and logo of Abdo Publishing.

Printed in the United States of America, North Mankato, Minnesota

02014
012015

Cover Photos: James Steidl/Shutterstock Images; Shutterstock Images
Interior Photos: James Steidl/Shutterstock Images, 1, 3; Shutterstock Images, 1, 3, 29; SuperStock/Glow Images, 7, 86; Science Faction/Glow Images, 9; Heritage Images/Glow Images, 12; Iberfoto/SuperStock, 15; Gianni Dagli Orti/Corbis, 17; iStockphoto, 20, 33, 81, 89, 96; Photos.com/Thinkstock, 22, 25, 26, 42, 44, 46; Interfoto/Alamy, 31; Tetra Images/SuperStock, 35; The Print Collector/Alamy, 36; Heritage Images/Corbis, 51; Bettmann/Corbis, 39, 55, 59, 61, 73, 79, 95; Everett Collection/SuperStock, 57; Science and Society/SuperStock, 63, 83; American Institute of Physics/AP Images, 65; National Geographic Image Collection/Alamy, 69; Harvard University Archives, 71; Burger/Phanie/SuperStock, 75; Corbis, 77; Dean Curtis/The Springfield News-Leader/AP Images, 93

Editor: Melissa York
Series Designer: Craig Hinton

Library of Congress Control Number: 2014943870

Cataloging-in-Publication Data
Roberts, Russell.
Medicine: a matter of life and death / Russell Roberts.
p. cm. -- (History of science)
ISBN 978-1-62403-563-0 (lib. bdg.)
Includes bibliographical references and index.
1. Medicine--History--Juvenile literature. I. Title.
610.9--dc23

2014943870

Contents

Chapter One   Life and Death 6

Chapter Two   Medicine Begins 16

Chapter Three   The Power of Observation 28

Chapter Four   Fighting Illness 38

Chapter Five   Relieving Pain 50

Chapter Six   Seeing Inside 60

Chapter Seven   Chickens and Frogs
Advance Medicine 68

Chapter Eight   Beautiful Mold 80

Chapter Nine   Medicine Marches On 88

TIMELINE 98
ESSENTIAL FACTS 100
GLOSSARY 102
ADDITIONAL RESOURCES 104
SOURCE NOTES 106
INDEX 110
ABOUT THE AUTHOR 112

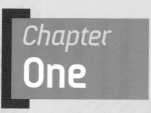

Life and DEATH

$$\frac{a+b}{a} = \frac{a}{b} = 1.618$$

The feverish young woman lying on the hospital cot weakly waved her arm at the half-filled glass of water held by the nurse. The nurse raised the glass to the woman's lips. The young woman struggled to raise her head and drank, then collapsed back onto the cot.

The nurse put down the glass and grabbed a towel soaking in a pan of water. She gently dabbed the young woman's brow and cheeks. The tropical air of Havana, Cuba, in August was thick and humid, only adding to the woman's distress.

The woman groaned in pain and shifted her body on the cot, trying to find a comfortable position, but her efforts were futile. She had yellow fever, and it was unlikely she would know comfort again. Her name was Clara Maass, and she was 24 years old.

An artist imagines the doctors who fought yellow fever in Cuba, including a volunteer being bitten by an infected mosquito.

YELLOW FEVER, SCOURGE OF HUMANITY

Some called yellow fever *vomito negro*—the black vomit—because blood leaking from the stomach mixed with digestive juices and became black. Others called it *yellow jack* because of the yellow quarantine flag flown in infected cities or on ships, warning others to stay away. Whatever it was called, it was deadly. In Philadelphia in 1793, it killed 5,000, approximately 10 percent of the city's residents.[1] At the height of the outbreak in 1878, the illness killed 90 to 100 people per day each in Memphis, Tennessee, New Orleans, Louisiana, and Vicksburg, Mississippi.[2] Until the early 1900s, no one knew what caused it or how to cure it.

It was August 23, 1901. Havana was experiencing a terrible yellow fever epidemic. Dr. William Gorgas, the city's chief sanitation officer, had issued a desperate call for nurses to tend to the overwhelming number of Havana's sick. Maass, a nurse from New Jersey, had answered the call.

Researchers in Havana were trying to figure out what caused yellow fever. They were narrowing in on the *Aedes aegypti* mosquito as a carrier of the disease. They needed human subjects to test whether having the disease once provided immunity in the future. Researchers sought volunteers who would be bitten by mosquitoes that had fed on yellow fever victims. The volunteers were offered $100 upfront and another $100 if they got the disease.

Nineteen people volunteered. Maass was the only American and the only woman in the group. She might have hoped she would get a mild case of yellow fever, recover, and become immune to the disease, which would make her a more effective nurse. She was bitten on several occasions between March and June 1901. She got a mild case of yellow fever and recovered. It was uncertain whether one bite was

Research in the early 1900s proved the mosquito origin of yellow fever.

enough to immunize her, so on August 14, 1901, she was again bitten by a mosquito suspected of carrying yellow fever.

The disease hit her hard the second time around. It tore through the young woman with all its horrendous symptoms—high fever, blood-soaked vomit, violent headaches, and extreme muscle pain.

"Pray for me," Maass wrote home in a shaky hand.[3]

In the sweltering hospital room in Havana, Maass groaned loudly and froze in place. The doctor rushed over upon hearing the nurse's cries and felt for Maass's pulse. It was feeble but still present. He nodded to the anxious nurse, who breathed a sigh of relief. But the worst was still to come. Maass died the following day, August 24, 1901.

Her death was not in vain. It proved the *Aedes aegypti* mosquito was indeed the carrier of yellow fever, ending the human experiments. Gorgas and others immediately began working toward eradicating the insect and its breeding areas.

CLARA MAASS

Clara Louise Maass was born in East Orange, New Jersey, on June 28, 1876. She was the first child of German immigrants Robert and Hedwig Maass. Eight more children followed, and money grew tight for the family. Clara began working while still in grammar school. In 1893, she enrolled in the nursing program at Newark German Hospital in Newark, New Jersey. Two years later she received her nursing cap and pin. Maass eventually became the hospital's head nurse.

Maass served as a nurse with the US Army in the Spanish-American War (1898) and was stationed in Florida, Georgia, and Cuba. In early 1900, she volunteered to go to the Philippines to help soldiers struck down by yellow fever. She was already very familiar with the disease when she returned to Cuba late in 1900.

Gorgas said, "Large sums of money and many lives have been saved, and will yearly be saved, by this discovery of the manner of propagation of yellow fever."[4]

Maass paid the ultimate price for her part in the research, but her death saved thousands of others who would have died from yellow fever. Honored on postage stamps and by a hospital named in her honor, the case of Maass proves once again that medicine has always been a matter of life and death.

Ancient Medicine

Ever since the first medicine man in the first primitive tribe treated sickness, medicine has saved lives that would have been lost without treatment. Surgery has been practiced since prehistoric times. Human skulls from 10,000 years ago have been found cut with a round piece of bone removed, a process called trepanation. Possibly done as a ritual or as a cure for headaches, new bone growth around the hole indicates the procedure was done skillfully enough that some people survived.

STRANGE MEDICINE

Many medical practices of ancient times look strange to modern eyes. But in their own time, they represented the healers' medical worldview, cultural knowledge, and sincere desire to cure their patients. In ancient Babylon, priests had their patients breathe into a sheep's nose. They then killed the sheep, examined its liver, stuck wooden pegs into a clay model of the liver, and predicted the patient's outcome.

Cataracts—a clouding of the lens in the eye—were treated in ancient Egypt by pouring hot broken glass into the eye. Patients with gout had to stand on an electric eel. Those growing bald received a potion containing a dog's toes. Egyptian doctors treated a toothache by stuffing a dead mouse down the patient's throat.

In Greece, physicians treated serious spinal curvature by throwing patients off tall buildings. One physician tried to straighten a patient's deformed back by placing three large stones on his spine. "He was crushed and died," someone wrote, "but he became straighter than a ruler."[5]

11

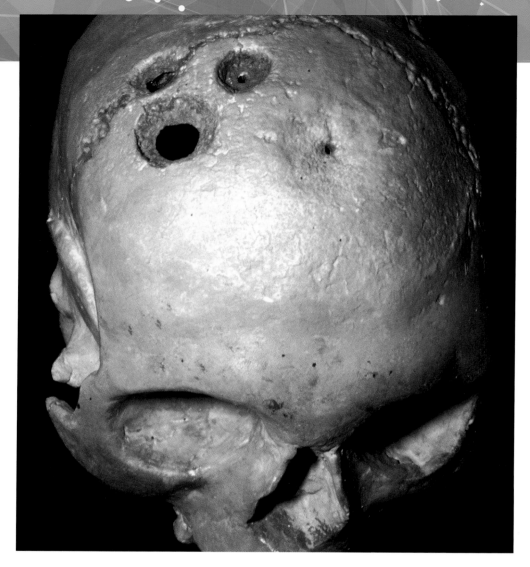

This ancient man survived his first trepanation long enough for the wound to partially close, *front right*, but later operations killed him.

In ancient Egypt, religious practice emphasized the importance of preserving bodies after death. As part of the mummification process, physicians removed internal organs. The physicians studied these organs, broadening humankind's knowledge of anatomy. Egyptian doctors also used herbs, minerals, and animal substances in their practices, which were made into salves, pills, and powders.

Throughout the ages, medicine—from the Latin *ars medicina*, "the art of healing"—has been both maddeningly backward and extraordinarily progressive. For every amazing advance that propels the field forward, there are examples of lifesaving innovations ignored in favor of conservative, traditional practices. The story of medical progress has been the story of those who dared seek something better, knowing there is no rest in the battle between life and death.

Women in Medicine

Women have played a role in medicine for centuries. It is likely women were healers in ancient civilizations such as Egypt and Babylon. Although early medical texts based on Greek thought held that women were a weaker version of men, women continued to slowly infiltrate medicine. By the end of the 1300s, Germany had 15 licensed female doctors.

Although women in professional medicine were considered taboo for a long time, midwifery was one field in which female practitioners were more accepted than men. Unfortunately, male physicians' guarding of medical education sometimes hurt patients. Elizabeth Cellier found that in England in the 1600s, two-thirds of the deaths related to childbirth and abortion were due to a midwife's lack of knowledge.[6]

Early in the 1800s, the Philadelphia County Medical Society declared women unfit for medicine "due to their delicate organization and predominance of the nervous system."[7] Elizabeth Blackwell was the first woman to attend medical school in the United States, graduating in 1849. Blackwell, her sister Emily, Marie Zakrzewska, and Mary Putnam Jacobi were other pioneering women in medicine during the 1800s in the United States.

Women continued breaking down the barriers as the 1900s progressed. In 1915, women were made full members of the American Medical Association. The Medical Women's National Association was formed that same year. Today, there are thousands of female physicians, nurses, researchers, and scientists in medicine. They are a vital part of the medical profession.

Medieval midwives assist a woman in labor.

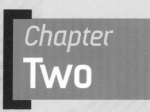

Chapter

Two

MEDICINE BEGINS

Many credit the beginnings of Western medical thought with the Greeks, particularly the physician Hippocrates. Often called the father of Western medicine, Hippocrates and other Greeks developed the concept of the four humors, or fluids: black bile, yellow bile, blood, and phlegm. When these were in balance in the body, they created *crasis* or *eucrasia*—perfect health. An imbalance of one or more caused *dyscrasia*, or poor health.

Clarissimus Galenus, commonly known as Galen, was an important figure in ancient medicine. Galen was born in approximately 130 CE in Pergamum, a Greek city in modern-day Turkey. He studied medicine in Smyrna (today in Turkey) and Alexandria, Egypt. At the time, human dissection was not permitted, but Galen wanted to have a better understanding of human anatomy. He returned home to Greece and began dissecting animals. He then went to Rome, Italy, where he served for a time as a physician to the gladiators. He was eventually considered the leading medical figure of his time.

Ancient Greek art holds clues about Greek doctors and medicine.

HIPPOCRATES

Another giant of Greek medicine, Hippocrates was born in 460 BCE on the Greek island of Cos. He is believed to have studied medicine under his father, Heracleides, and traveled to the Greek mainland, Egypt, and Libya to observe medical practices.

Hippocrates taught that disease was a natural process—not a divine act—and the physician was a man of science. He advised doctors to use their powers of observation, taught that broken bones needed to be aligned correctly to heal properly, and said the body could often heal itself naturally. Hippocrates died in approximately 375 BCE. According to legend, Hippocrates or one of his students wrote the Hippocratic Oath, a promise doctors still make today to heal all patients to the best of their ability.

Constantly seeking to advance his knowledge, Galen studied the muscles, spinal cord, heart, and urinary system. He proved arteries were full of blood. He experimented on a living dog to study the bladder and urine flow. He is often credited with introducing experimentation into medicine. A relentless researcher and writer, he claimed to have written 125 books on numerous subjects.[1] It is said he sometimes kept several scribes busy at the same time writing down his thoughts, observations, and conclusions.

Galen wasn't always right. He believed women and men were identical, but the female reproductive system was turned in while a man's was turned out. He believed blood originated in the liver and moved back and forth through the body, passing through the heart. Even though much of Galen's work was lost after the fall of the Roman Empire and the rise of the Middle Ages (400–1400 CE), his reputation was so great—he was called "The Prince of Physicians"—that his findings and conclusions were considered sacred and dominated medical thought for 15 centuries.

Church Medicine

During the Middle Ages in Europe, culture, government, and science, including medicine, all looked to the Catholic Church. Monk scribes copied and recopied ancient Latin texts, including works on medicine. The church preached faith healing, meaning shrines, religious objects, and saints were used to heal the sick. People prayed to Saint Dymphna for mental illness, Saint Roch for plague, Saint Blaise for throat ailments, and others for other complaints. Doctors who tried to treat patients by their own methods could be accused of interfering with God's plan. However, sometimes the sick were directed to secular methods for treating illness, such as using wine to help treat wounds.

Christian clergy were not permitted to perform surgery. Barbers performed small surgical procedures, such as tooth extraction, blood-letting, and other minor operations. Surgeons handled more complex medical tasks, such as battlefield medicine and amputations.

Astrology played a major part in medieval medicine, even though it was associated with magic, which had been banned by the church. It was thought the alignment of the planets determined the best time to treat a patient. Most doctors knew the exact time to prescribe a specific treatment, based on the movement and position of planets and stars.

Arabic medicine, which had a strong influence on European medicine, held that different zodiac signs controlled specific body parts. Medical charts contained information on what not to do for those born under a specific sign; for example, doctors were advised to avoid cutting the feet of a Pisces or the belly of a Virgo. English philosopher Roger Bacon (1214–1294) believed a doctor ignorant of astronomy owed the effectiveness of his treatment to luck. "It is manifest [clear] to everyone that celestial bodies are the cause of generation and corruption in all things," he said.[2]

Sanitation Nightmare and the Black Death

One of the biggest losses of Roman knowledge concerned sanitation in cities. The technical expertise Roman engineers used to build sewers and aqueducts was forgotten. More and more people were moving into already overcrowded cities. Residents simply threw their garbage and sewage out the door or window of their dwelling, often without looking to see if anyone was in their line of fire. Country people who moved to the city brought cattle, hogs, and other animals with them. These farm animals roamed the city alongside rodents and vermin, feasting on the garbage they could find everywhere.

A history-changing crisis demonstrated the complete helplessness of medieval medicine: the Black Death. Plague had been around for centuries. Rome had been

A medieval doctor extracts a tooth.

Religious ceremonies and processions were useless in stopping the plague.

struck by epidemics of bubonic plague in 68, 79, 125, and 164 CE. But in both its reach and its randomness, the Black Death was a horribly lethal killer. From 1347 to 1350, historians estimate the Black Death killed as much as 25 percent of Europe's population.[3] It killed nearly 75 percent of the population of Florence, Italy, between 1338 and 1447.[4] People avoided those with the plague at all costs. "Charity was dead and hope abandoned," said French surgeon Guy de Chauliac.[5]

Physicians were helpless in the face of this onslaught of death. "It was useless and shameful for the physicians, especially because they did not care to visit the sick for fear of becoming themselves afflicted, and if they visited them, they gave nothing," wrote de Chauliac.[6] Considering the remedies prescribed, sometimes doing nothing was actually better. Strong odors were thought to counteract the Black Death, so people were told to stand over a latrine for hours and breathe in the smell. Fires were lit in the streets to clear the air. People were bled and made to vomit, which just weakened them.

Yet the beginnings of the public health movement can be seen in the actions communities took to try to stop the Black Death, such as airing homes, controlling water supplies, and preventing suspected plague carriers from entering cities. And there were other pinpoints of medical light during these times. In the 800s, one of the first European medical schools began in Salerno, Italy. A medical text from Salerno, Surgery of Rogerius, was written in 1170 by Rogerius

PHLEBOTOMY—A BLOODY BUSINESS

Blood-letting was a popular medical treatment throughout the Middle Ages and for centuries after. It was seen as ridding the body of excess or bad blood that caused illness.

One blood-letting method, called phlebotomy or venesection, involved opening a vein. Another method was to place leeches above a cut and let them suck on the "bad" blood below. Leeches contain a substance called hirudin, which prevents clotting and keeps the blood flowing. Leeches are still used in medicine today to remove extra blood and help healing, such as when a finger or ear has been reattached.

Salernitanus. It is considered the first widely used surgical textbook in the Western world. Then, in 1543, Andreas Vesalius kick-started the age of modern medicine.

The Studies of Andreas Vesalius

Andreas Vesalius was born in Brussels, Belgium, in 1514. As a medical student, Vesalius was disgusted with the teaching of human anatomy in Paris, France, which consisted of the professor reading Galen, dissecting some animals, and showing a few easily accessible parts of the human body. He felt that for physicians to really know the body they had to actually dissect it, something that was infrequently done at the time because a dissected body could not have a regular funeral or burial. His desire to experiment, using his own hands, foreshadowed the coming scientific revolution and its insistence on first-hand observation.

Vesalius began prowling the Cemetery of the Innocents in Paris, digging up dead bodies and sometimes even fighting with wild dogs over body parts. He went to an area where the bodies of executed criminals were hung, cut them down, and took them home. He stored these rotting corpses in his bedroom, sometimes for weeks on end, so he could cut them up and examine them.

All of this effort gave Vesalius so much knowledge of the human body he was named head of the Department of Surgery and Anatomy at the University of Padua

PARACELSUS

Born in 1493 in Switzerland, revolutionary doctor Philippus Aureolus Theophrastus Bombastus von Hohenheim—known as Paracelsus—learned medicine as a boy from his father. He then wandered as far as Sweden, Egypt, Russia, and England, learning medicine from official outlets in universities and from barbers, astrologers, midwives, and other underground sources. About current doctors he said, "Even the flies would disdain to sit on them except to make their dirt."[7] He once opened a lecture by building a bonfire to burn the works of Galen.

He understood mental illness was caused by disease, not demons. He urged doctors to understand what made medicines effective instead of just making potions because of tradition. With a strong interest in alchemy, he also applied his knowledge of chemicals to medical treatment. He criticized physicians who blindly accepted ancient teachings, particularly Galen. He died from injuries received in a brawl in 1541.

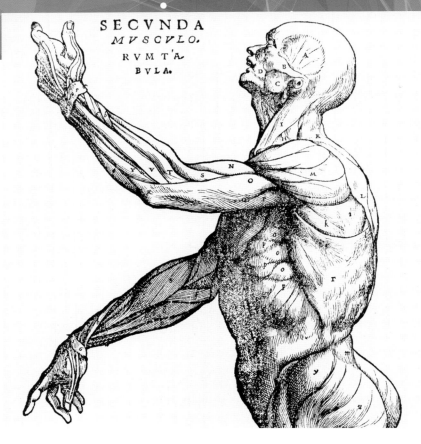

Vesalius's anatomy drawings were the most precise and accurate of his day.

in Italy at age 23. His interesting, informative lectures, illustrated with charts and drawings, attracted hundreds of people. At first he balanced his talks between what he knew to be true and what the ancient physician Galen had said. But in 1538, he printed and offered for sale six charts in which he slightly criticized Galen. They sold quickly, encouraging Vesalius to put forward his discoveries.

Vesalius spent the next five years working on a book that was finally published in 1543. Titled *De Humani Corporis Fabrica* (*On the Fabric of the Human Body*), the book and its more than 200 illustrations created a sensation when it appeared. Today considered a groundbreaking medical text that provided the first accurate portrayal of human anatomy, the book was not universally appreciated at first. Indeed, some wanted Vesalius punished for daring to contradict the great Galen.

The growing criticism so bothered Vesalius that in the last days of 1543 he made a large pile of his notes and papers and burned them. He left Padua and became physician to Holy Roman Emperor Charles V in Madrid, Spain. He then lived in Jerusalem for a time, but on a voyage back to Italy he was shipwrecked on the Greek island of Zante. He died there in 1564 of starvation and exposure. But his ideas lived on. The new scientific study of human anatomy had pried open the door of medical progress that had been closed for many centuries. A cautious Englishman would soon tear that door off its hinges.

BATTLEFIELD DOCTOR

Ambroise Paré was born in 1510 in France. The son of a barber, he apprenticed as a barber-surgeon, and in 1537 he served in his first military campaign in Turin. When he ran out of boiling oil, the accepted method for treating gunshot wounds, he made a solution of egg yolk, rose oil, and turpentine and put it on the soldiers' wounds. These soldiers felt little pain the next day, while those treated with oil were in agony.

Paré's most important discovery, however, was that bleeding after amputations could be stopped by tying the blood vessels with cord instead of using red-hot cauterization. He saved so many lives on the battlefield with his revolutionary treatment of wounds that soldiers carried him on their shoulders in gratitude. "I dressed the wound and God healed him," Paré said.[8] He died in 1590.

The Power of
OBSERVATION

A ncient people were aware of the heart's importance to the human body. They knew that once it stopped beating, life ended. However, because they only examined the hearts of corpses, they did not understand how blood circulates. Today doctors know blood is pumped from the arteries through the body, returning to the heart via veins. When the heart stops beating, the arteries contract and push all their blood into the veins. The ancients saw empty arteries and thought they contained only air.

Galen made several important discoveries about the heart, realizing it is essentially a muscle. He also found that arteries carried blood, not air. He theorized that blood seeped into the arteries through pores in the membrane that divided the heart's right and left sides.

$$\frac{a+b}{a} = \frac{a}{b} = 1.618$$

Modern technology allows today's doctors much greater understanding of circulation and other body processes.

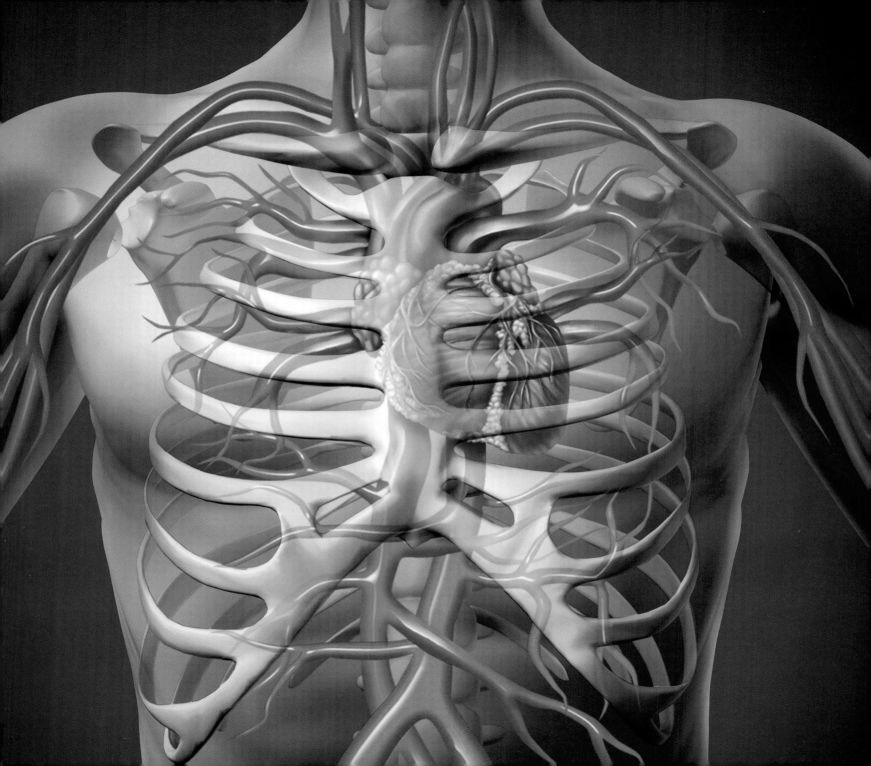

ISLAMIC MEDICINE AND IBN AN-NAFIS

Medieval Islamic scientists and doctors kept more knowledge of ancient medicine and science alive than their European counterparts. Islamic scholars preserved ancient texts, and their translations and commentaries proved invaluable to the late medieval revival of European medicine. During the Middle Ages, Islamic doctors practiced more scientific and observation-based medicine than Europeans. One of these revolutionary doctors was Ibn an-Nafis. Born in 1213 near Damascus, Syria, Nafis was active in many fields, including physiology, ophthalmology, psychology, philosophy, law, and theology. He wrote that it was not possible for blood to flow directly from one side of the heart to the other and that the heart did not contain pores that allowed blood to travel through, both long-accepted, incorrect Western views. He then described the circulation system in a way similar to what research would reveal several hundred years later. Despite the groundbreaking aspects of Ibn an-Nafis's work, it was not discovered by Western medicine until 1924 when his writings were uncovered in Berlin, Germany.

Scientists who followed Galen suspected this was incorrect. A Syrian physician in the 1200s, Ibn an-Nafis, found no evidence of pores. Neither did Vesalius. Instead, they believed blood circulated in the body. In the mid-1500s, Spanish doctor and philosopher Michael Servetus also wrote of circulation.

In 1559, the findings of Italian anatomist Realdo Colombo were published in *The 15 Books Written Concerning Anatomy*. By dissecting live animals and human cadavers, Columbo determined that blood circulated between the two sections of the heart through the lungs. Although the ancient Greek philosopher Aristotle had taught that the left portion of the heart contained cold blood and the right warm blood, Columbo disagreed. Through animal dissection, he found that blood in the veins traveled from the heart to the lungs, where it mixed with air before returning to the heart. In 1571, Italian botanist and physician Andreas Cesalpino expanded this theory, arguing that blood circulated throughout the body. The stage was now set for William Harvey.

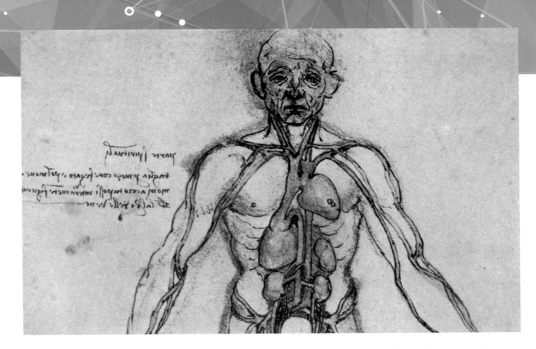

Artist and scientist Leonardo da Vinci made detailed drawings of arteries and veins in the 1400s but did not crack the secret of blood circulation.

William Harvey Describes Blood Circulation

William Harvey was born in 1578 at Folkestone, near Dover, England. He went to Padua for his medical training. This was the same school at which Colombo had taught, and it is possible Harvey became familiar with Colombo's work there.

Harvey began investigating the human heart. He did not want to dispute Galen, whom he considered a genius. "It is not in my nature to upset the established order," he once said.[1] He just wanted to learn about the relationship between the heart and arteries. He knew the only way to do this was by dissection and observation. First he dissected dead animals, and then he moved on to live test subjects, cutting them open and watching how their hearts worked. When the hearts of warm-blooded animals beat too fast for Harvey to observe them, he switched to cold-blooded animals such as fish, whose hearts beat slower. These methods paid off. In 1603, Harvey described his discovery: "The movement of the blood occurs constantly in a circular manner and is the result of the beating of the heart."[2]

Harvey tied off areas of a human upper arm and watched which parts of the arm turned pale from lack of blood. This helped him understand how blood traveled through the body. By using mathematical calculations, he realized the amount of blood the body required during one hour could not be produced by the liver. This destroyed the ancient idea that the liver produced blood. This was also the first time in medicine that scientific methods, in the form of calculations, were used to prove a theory. Harvey realized the heart was essentially a pump that constantly circulated blood throughout the body.

Paving the Way

Fully aware of how revolutionary his theories were, Harvey waited 12 years before publishing them. He spent the years lecturing to his colleagues about the heart, arteries, and veins. During these lectures, Harvey would cut open a living animal and

Harvey was the first scientist to suggest humans reproduced when a sperm fertilized an egg.

32

SURGERY AND THE SCIENTIFIC METHOD

John Hunter was the world's first experimental surgeon. Today he is considered the father of modern scientific surgery. His work continued Harvey's spirit of observation, measurement, and the scientific method. Hunter was born in 1728 in Lanarkshire, Scotland. He argued against surgeons acting too quickly and said an operation was a doctor's admission he could not heal the patient naturally. "To know the cause of the effects [of an illness] is the most important thing," he said.[4]

Nevertheless, Hunter was a skilled surgeon. While with the British army, Hunter rejected the then-common method of treating gunshot wounds by deliberately making them much bigger in order to remove the bullet. Instead, he devised less invasive treatments. He also developed a procedure to relieve distorted joints. Through continuous experimentation, he devised a new method to treat human aneurysms without amputation. Hunter repeatedly showed that only after experimentation should an operation take place. "Why not try the experiment?" was his philosophy.[5]

let his audience watch as the blood circulated. By the time he was ready to publish his findings, they had already been demonstrated for all to see. Harvey published a 72-page book entitled *Anatomical Studies on the Motion of the Heart and Blood* in 1628. Still worried how his work would be received, he wrote, "[My next words are] of so novel and unheard-of character, that I not only fear injury to myself from the envy of a few, but I tremble lest I have mankind at large for my enemies."[3]

After his book appeared, Harvey did indeed have his critics, including a French physician who admitted there might be some blood circulation through the heart but certainly not through the entire body. Yet by the time Harvey died in 1657, almost everyone accepted his discovery.

Harvey began the age of measurement in medicine. It was best demonstrated by Italian doctor Santorio Santorio, who invented instruments to measure temperature and pulse rate. The next great medical discovery, however, came not from a physician, but from a merchant.

Van Leeuwenhoek's small device gave greater magnification than previously possible.

The Invention of the Microscope

Although Roman writings from the first century CE refer to magnifying glasses, science learned little about magnification until near the end of the 1200s, when spectacles were invented. Then, in approximately 1590, Dutch spectacle maker Hans Jensen and his son Zacharias found that looking through several lenses arranged in a tube greatly enlarged objects. The device quickly became popular with scientists. In the 1670s, Dutch merchant Antonie van Leeuwenhoek developed new ways to grind

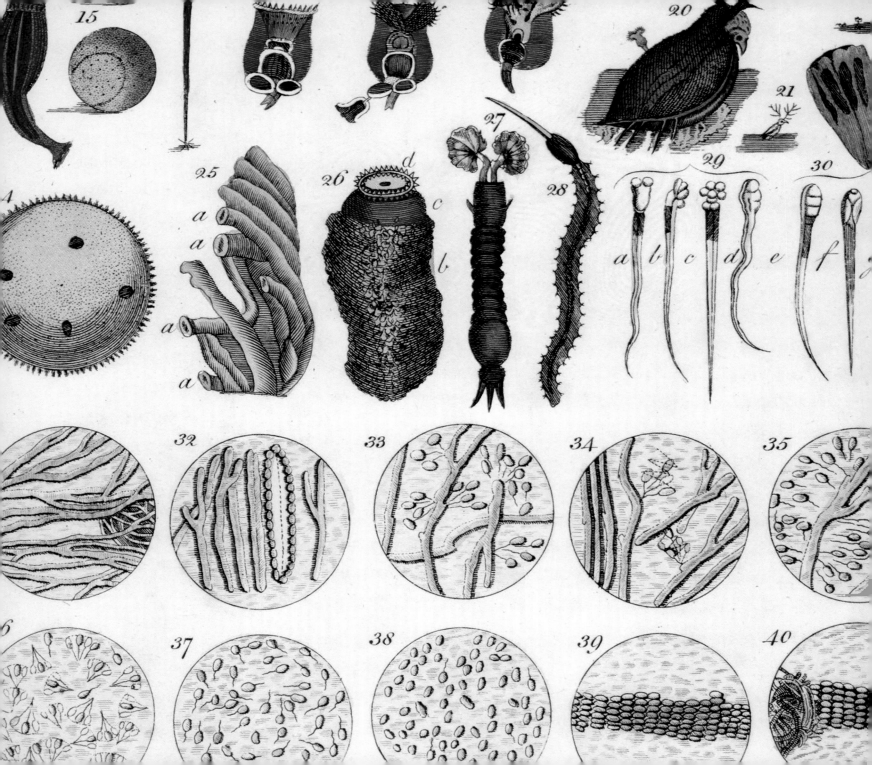

and polish tiny, curved lenses, thus producing much greater magnifications than had been possible before.

In October 1676, a letter from van Leeuwenhoek arrived at the Royal Society in London, England, containing the following statement: "I discovered little creatures in rain which had stood but a few days in a new tub."[6] His powerful microscopes had allowed him to see these "little creatures," or as they would be called today, bacteria.

Van Leeuwenhoek examined numerous things under his microscope, including scrapings from his teeth, his own feces, and animal dung. Sometimes, as when he examined the roots of his decayed tooth, he saw the little animals again. At these times, even though he wasn't a physician or scientist, he was close to understanding the connection between bacteria, germs, and disease, but he did not connect all the dots.

Several decades later, Austrian doctor Marc von Plenciz declared the "animalcules," as van Leeuwenhoek sometimes called them, were responsible for contagious diseases. However, many still refused to believe the world was populated by invisible microorganisms that could cause deadly diseases. A prime cause of disease was thought to be miasma gases and other unpleasant substances. Future discoveries would reveal the true sources behind the spread of disease.

Van Leeuwenhoek had illustrations made of the tiny creatures he saw in his microscope.

FIGHTING ILLNESS

Smallpox was one of the worst killers in recorded history. In the later half of the 1700s, one out of every ten people in Europe died of smallpox, and more than 50 percent of those were children.[1] Smallpox killed 20 to 40 percent of the people who got it.[2] Those who recovered often went blind or had their faces covered in pockmarks.

Physicians had been trying to cure smallpox for centuries. Some methods reflected an awareness that a person who had smallpox once could not get it again. Healers in ancient China ground up a smallpox scab taken from a survivor, then blew the dust up a person's nostrils—the left nostril for a man, the right for a woman. Arab physicians rubbed material from a smallpox blister in small incisions on the arm.

Inoculation was a folk remedy in parts of Europe. Inoculating specifically for smallpox is sometimes called variolation. People would have a party and invite a local healer, often an old woman, who was known to perform the service. She would make an incision in a person's arm and put smallpox material into the wound. The goal was

Smallpox threatened disfigurement and death around the world until relatively recently.

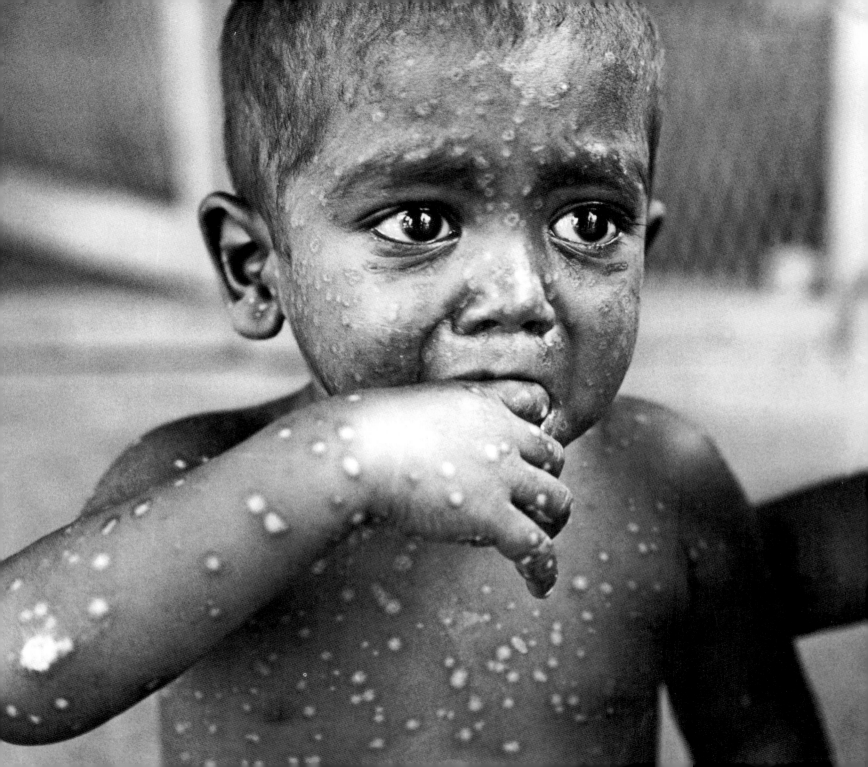

to contract a mild form of the disease to make the person immune to more serious forms. However, variolation was dangerous and could backfire. A low dose meant to cause immunity could instead turn out to be lethal, even triggering an epidemic.

In 1717, after smallpox destroyed her own legendary beauty, Lady Mary Wortley Montagu variolated her children with smallpox material, having learned about the procedure in Turkey. Her actions popularized variolation (from the Latin word *variola*, or smallpox) among the European aristocracy. By 1735, 850 people had experienced variolation in England.[3] More did not try it because English physicians had instituted a grueling six-week preparation period prior to the procedure in which patients were bled, placed on a low-calorie diet, and made to vomit constantly. Historians estimate 12 percent of those treated died—a measurement of how unpredictable variolation could be.[4] Since variolation was not widely accepted and the poor usually had little access to it, England's rate of smallpox infection actually got higher in the 1700s.

SMALLPOX WARFARE

Smallpox also came to the New World, ripping through native communities along with other deadly epidemics and devastating the population. Smallpox unintentionally helped Cortez defeat the Aztecs in Mexico in 1521. In 1763, smallpox was part of one of the first recorded uses of germ warfare. British General Jeffrey Amherst suggested smallpox be given to certain Native American tribes during Pontiac's War (1763–1764). The British army was subsequently billed by a private company for "[items] got to Replace . . . those which were taken from people in the Hospital to Convey the Small-pox to the Indians."[5]

Vaccination Advances

British surgeon Edward Jenner was all too familiar with smallpox, having been variolated himself at eight years old. During the brutal six-week preparation period, he was bled until he was pale, made to vomit, and denied solid food until he was skeleton thin. Only then was he treated.

As part of his training to become a surgeon, Jenner apprenticed with a country doctor. Sometime between 1763 and 1770, he was examining a milkmaid who had come down with cowpox. Humans often caught cowpox, which was similar to smallpox in appearance but usually caused just a few days' discomfort. As Jenner examined her, she said, "Now I'll never take the smallpox, for I have had the cowpox."[6]

MEDICINE IN COLONIAL AMERICA

By the 1700s, most of the American medical establishment still treated sickness by sweating, bleeding, blistering, and vomiting the patient, in accordance with the medical theories that were still predominant. Dung (both human and animal), urine, and various animal and plant material were prescribed. As one patient's "treatment" was described: "[The treatment] gave him 100 vomits and as many stools, brought the Convulsions on him, which soon carried him off, and caused him to purge till he was Interr'd [buried]."[7]

On December 14, 1799, after working outside at his Mount Vernon home in foul weather, former president George Washington developed a severe throat infection and had trouble breathing. He asked a plantation employee to bleed him—a treatment he believed in—and eight ounces (0.2 L) of blood were removed. The physicians in attendance bled Washington three more times, the last taking 32 ounces (0.9 L) of blood, produced a blister on his throat, and forced him to vomit, among other treatments.[8] Nothing helped, and Washington died that night. Historians speculate the medical treatments, particularly the bleeding, hastened the former president's death.

Jenner inoculated children with cowpox to protect them from smallpox.

Those words stayed with Jenner. He wondered if he could stop people from catching smallpox by inoculating them with cowpox. On December 17, 1789, he inoculated his ten-month-old son Edward Jr. and two other women with material taken from a swinepox sore (a disease similar to cowpox). All three got slightly sick but quickly recovered. Jenner then variolated the three with smallpox itself. Again, there was a slight sickness, but nothing more. Jenner variolated his son two more times, in December 1790 and December 1791, and the child did not get sick.

To further test his theory, in May 1796 Jenner inoculated eight-year-old James Phipps, the son of a laborer who worked for him, with cowpox. On July 1, Jenner then variolated the boy with smallpox. James did not catch the disease. These tests showed giving a healthy person cowpox could protect them against catching smallpox. Jenner called his procedure *vaccinae*, related to the Latin *vacca*, "cow." Other doctors took up the practice, and vaccination replaced variolation as the preferred means of preventing smallpox. Vaccines for many diseases followed. In 1980, the World Health Organization declared smallpox eradicated around the world.

The Germ Theory of Disease

Medical experiments throughout the 1800s pushed forward human understanding of disease. No one better demonstrated the growing bond between medicine and science than Louis Pasteur. He was a chemist, not a doctor, yet his discoveries saved millions of lives. He was born on December 27, 1822, in France, the son of a tanner.

In 1854, Pasteur was in Lille, France. A man named Bigot who owned a factory that produced alcohol from sugar beets asked him why the alcohol was sometimes good and why it was sometimes sour and foul tasting. Using his microscope and his scientific skills, Pasteur found that good alcohol contained a round microbe, but a rod-shaped microbe was always present in the foul liquid. After conducting experiments, Pasteur found that heating the wine to a temperature of 131 degrees

Fahrenheit (55°C) destroyed the harmful bacteria but did not damage the wine. This process became known as pasteurization, and it is still used today.

Most important for medicine, Pasteur declared that bad microorganisms carried contagious diseases that caused sickness and death in humans and animals. The old belief of spontaneous generation held that life could develop from decaying plant or animal matter. It was spontaneous generation, for example, that explained why maggots appeared on rotting meat. Spontaneous generation was cited as a reason for disease, and it was believed rotting material spontaneously generated bad air, which spread via miasmas. Pasteur conducted an experiment in which he boiled two bottles of fluid to remove all microorganisms. He covered one but not the other. Life did not develop in the covered flask, but it did in the one exposed to the air. This experiment helped Pasteur disprove spontaneous generation.

In 1865, after his success with wine, the French government asked Pasteur to investigate the silkworm industry. A disease was attacking the silkworms, and the industry had seen revenues plunge from $5 million to a few hundred thousand dollars per year.[9] Pasteur worked on the problem for five years. He found two separate diseases, caused by two different microbes, were killing the silkworms, and elimination of these microbes would stop the disease. Again, he had proven microbes cause disease.

Pasteur's work advanced understanding of bacteria and disease.

Robert KOCH

Born on December 11, 1843, in Clausthal, Hannover, Germany, biologist Robert Koch provided the definitive proof of Pasteur's work that bacteria was the cause, and not the consequence, of infection. In 1880, after proving beyond question that anthrax was caused by a specific microbe, Koch was called to Berlin, Germany, to work with a group of assistants tracking down disease-causing bacteria. They succeeded in identifying the microbes that caused diseases such as gonorrhea, diphtheria, typhoid fever, gangrene, leprosy, and tetanus.

Perhaps Koch's greatest achievement was discovering the cause of tuberculosis. He identified the bacterial cause of the disease and demonstrated that it could be diagnosed by finding traces of it in sputum (material ejected from the lungs via the mouth). This allowed physicians to diagnose, and eventually treat, the disease. Koch won the Nobel Prize in 1905.

Safer Surgeries

British surgeon Joseph Lister embraced Pasteur's ideas. In February 1874, Lister wrote Pasteur a letter. He said his own groundbreaking success in preventing surgical infection was the result of Pasteur's germ theory. Lister wrote, "Your brilliant researches demonstrated the truth of the germ theory of putrefaction and thus having furnished me with the principle upon which the antiseptic system can be carried out."[10]

Lister was born in Essex, England, in 1827. In 1861, as head of Glasgow's Royal Infirmary, he witnessed a large number of infected surgical wounds, which was considered a routine consequence of operations. Surgeons would wear operating coats stiff with dried blood and body fluids from previous procedures. Their knives were often dirty and stained. Any instruments they used to examine patients were caked with dried fluids from other patients. They used ordinary needle and thread to close incisions and stuck the needles in the lapels of their coats for the next use.

THE RISE OF PUBLIC HEALTH

New discoveries about infectious diseases made it clear one person's health and cleanliness affected other people. In 1854, John Snow showed that only people who drank from a certain infected water pump in London came down with cholera. Other scientists also showed contaminated water to be a disease carrier. Gradually, it became clear how necessary clean water and sewage removal were to health.

Prominent medical personnel in England popularized the idea the health of the individual is inevitably connected with the health of the general public. This idea took root in the United States through New York City's 1866 passage of the Metropolitan Health Act, which became the model for public health agencies in other US cities and states. The bill removed responsibility for city sewage and sanitation from city hall and placed it under a new board of health. Some of the unhealthy conditions that led to the bill's passage were streets filled with piles of manure, sewer lines not connected to the main sewer, privies unconnected to sewers, and dirty pools of stagnant water everywhere.

THE HAZARDS OF CHILDBIRTH

Historically, the medical establishment—consisting almost exclusively of men—has misunderstood medical problems specific to women. Childbirth was particularly dangerous and often deadly. Through medieval times, childbirth was left to midwives, and 10 percent of women died during or soon after delivery.[12]

By the 1600s, medical students were making some deliveries in hospitals. However, because these doctors did not wash their hands, infection and disease were rampant among new mothers. In 1847, Hungarian obstetrician Ignaz Philipp Semmelweis—pre-dating Lister—ordered that all attendants of women in labor must first wash their hands in calcium chloride before attending to patients. This immediately reduced the mortality rate in his department from 12 percent to near zero.[13]

Lister knew the idea of miasma causing infections was wrong. After learning of Pasteur's germ theory, he decided to use carbolic acid, a weak acid, as a disinfectant during his surgeries. After some experimentation, the first test came on August 12, 1865, on 11-year-old James Greenlees, who had suffered a compound fracture of his left leg when a cart ran over it. Lister took a piece of lint, dipped it in carbolic acid, and then applied it to Greenlees's injury. The wound, which would likely have become infected under standard treatment, stayed clean and ultimately healed. Lister continued using a carbolic acid solution, cleaning instruments and washing hands with it and spraying it in the operating room.

The success of Lister's methods was plain. The fatality rate for his surgical patients between 1867 and 1870—after he introduced his new procedure—plunged from 45.7 percent to 15 percent.[11] Lister had devised the medical process of antisepsis, the local destruction of bacteria. However, there were many doctors, especially in the United States, who clung to the old ways. In 1876, Lister toured the United States and presented his findings but found many skeptics. Prominent surgeon Samuel Gross declared, "The honor, the dignity and the glory of American surgery will be safe" without Lister's methods.[14]

There were problems with Lister's method. The carbolic acid irritated the skin, causing doctors to experience bleached, numb skin and cracked nails. Breathing in the spray irritated the lungs, and in extreme cases it could cause poisoning. By 1886, steam and boric acid (which Lister himself eventually used) were being used for antiseptic purposes instead. But it all started with Lister and his willingness to try something new. By 1910, the death rate from amputation, which had been approximately 40 percent before Lister's discoveries, had dropped to less than 3 percent. Even Pasteur said that Lister "has done the most for suffering humanity."[15]

AMERICAN MEDICAL ATTITUDES

In the mid-1800s, many medical schools in the United States had woefully inadequate courses of study. Many medical "schools" sold diplomas through the mail; all a student had to do was send money to receive a medical degree. Bleeding was the main treatment prescribed. One doctor said he could float a steamboat on all of the blood he had drawn from his patients.

Ironically, some of the principles upon which the United States was based—including the admiration of the common man and suspicion of an educated upper class—affected medical development in the country. The feeling was that almost anyone had the right to be a physician and practice medicine. Unfortunately, this produced many fakes and quacks in the field who proclaimed themselves "doctors."

RELIEVING PAIN

Surgery before the development of anesthesia was a nightmare. Hospitals typically were designed with the operating room on the top floor so that patients' screams would not rise throughout the building. When an operation was ready to be performed, the thick door to the room was closed to muffle screaming. Battlefield surgery, which during the 1800s included many amputations, was often even more traumatic.

Hospital surgeries were often performed in operating theaters, with seats available for spectators. The famous naturalist Charles Darwin spoke of watching two operations when he was young but rushing away in horror before they were finished. Years later the memory of those experiences still haunted him. By necessity, an operation and a surgeon had to be quick because the patient could not survive a lengthy procedure. Some surgeons, including Robert Liston of England, became famous for their lightning-speed operations. Students brought stopwatches to surgeries so they could time them.

Surgery without anesthesia was brutal and by necessity short.

Facing Pain

Although ideas about pain relief had been present for centuries—the first to use the word *anesthesia* was the ancient Greek army surgeon Dioscorides—little had been done to advance the concept. In the Middle Ages in Europe, pain was viewed as being in accordance with God's wishes. Even in 1591, a Scottish woman named Eufane MacAyane was buried alive for asking for pain relief during a difficult childbirth. As late as 1847, the clergy of Edinburgh, Scotland, was still horrified at the thought of pain relief, saying, "To all seeming, Satan wishes to help suffering women, but the upshot will be the collapse of society, for the fear of the Lord, which depends on the petitions of the afflicted, will be destroyed."[1]

Doctors tried herbs, alcohol, ice, nerve clamping, and even hypnotism to relieve surgical pain, all without success. This led many to hold the same view as noted French surgeon Alfred Velpeau in 1839: "To escape pain in surgical operations is a chimera [illusion] which we are not permitted to look for in our day."[2]

Early Uses of Anesthesia

Some substances with anesthetic properties were used for other purposes for many years before their pain-relieving qualities were fully studied and appreciated. As far back as 1275, Spanish alchemist Raymundus Lullius discovered what he called sweet vitriol. This substance, now known as ether, is a highly flammable liquid that doctors first used as a medicine. Later users discovered ether can mask pain if it is vaporized.

In 1772, English chemist Joseph Priestly discovered nitrous oxide. At the dawn of the 1800s, the surgeon and chemist Humphrey Davy published a landmark book on nitrous oxide. He called the substance "laughing gas" because people who inhaled it became giddy. He also noted how it could be used as surgical anesthesia. But his recommendation was ignored.

A few years later, in 1808, William Barton from the University of Pennsylvania in the United States echoed Davy's comments. But advances in the use of nitrous oxide for medical purposes slowed, in part because the gas was being used for entertainment. Everyone from high society members to students seeking cheap thrills inhaled the gas. It caused giggling, laughing, aimless wandering, and sometimes even unconsciousness.

Surgical Anesthesia

In early 1842, some friends asked Georgia physician and surgeon Crawford Long to get them some laughing gas for a party. He gave them ether instead, and he and his friends blissfully stumbled through the hours. Later, when he had regained his senses, Long realized he could not remember feeling any pain even though he was bruised from smashing into things.

A patient of Long's, James Venable, had canceled several surgeries for the removal of two cysts because he was scared of the pain. Long thought ether might be the answer. On March 30, 1842, Long had Venable inhale ether until he was unconscious then removed one of the cysts. When Venable awoke, he did not believe Long had removed the cyst until the doctor showed it to him.

Long used ether in several other surgical applications with similar results. However, he did not publish his findings until 1849, seven years later. This delay helped fuel an argument that continues to this day.

The Anesthesia Controversy

On December 10, 1844, dentist Horace Wells attended a laughing gas exhibition at Union Hall in Hartford, Connecticut, put on by Professor Gardner Colton. Watching people stumble into things without experiencing pain gave him an idea. The next day, he arranged for Colton to give him nitrous oxide before allowing an assistant to

Crawford Long was among the first doctors to use ether as an anesthetic during surgery.

pull a bad tooth from his mouth. Realizing that the gas could be medically helpful, Wells then went to Boston, Massachusetts, and asked his former partner, Dr. William Morton, to arrange a demonstration in front of Dr. John Collins Warren's class at Harvard Medical School. But something went wrong during the demonstration and the patient screamed. Wells was ridiculed out of the room by the students.

Meanwhile, at the suggestion of chemist Dr. Charles T. Jackson, Morton replaced the nitrous oxide with ether and used it to painlessly remove a patient's bad tooth.

Morton arranged another demonstration with Warren. This one took place on October 16, 1846, in the same amphitheater where Wells had failed. Warren surgically removed a tumor, with Morton supplying the anesthesia. The operation took 25 minutes and was performed in complete silence. After it was over, Warren proclaimed, "Gentlemen, this is no humbug."[4]

Congress proposed an award of $100,000 to be paid to the discoverer of painless surgery.[5] A bitter battle between Jackson and Morton erupted over who was first to discover surgical anesthesia, with Long and Wells's widow as occasional participants. The debate raged for 16 years and has never been resolved. The award remains unpaid.

Civil War Medicine

During the American Civil War (1861–1865), surviving a battle was no guarantee of surviving the war. It is estimated the ratio of battle deaths to disease was approximately one in three in the Confederacy (5,000 killed in battle would equal 15,000 dead from sickness and disease) and approximately one in two for the Union (5,000 killed in battle would equal 10,000 dead from sickness and disease).[6] "We operated in our pus-stained coats," said one surgeon. "We used undisinfected instruments. . . . Surgeons . . . nearly always imperiled life and often actually caused death."[7]

Morton demonstrated painless surgery in 1846.

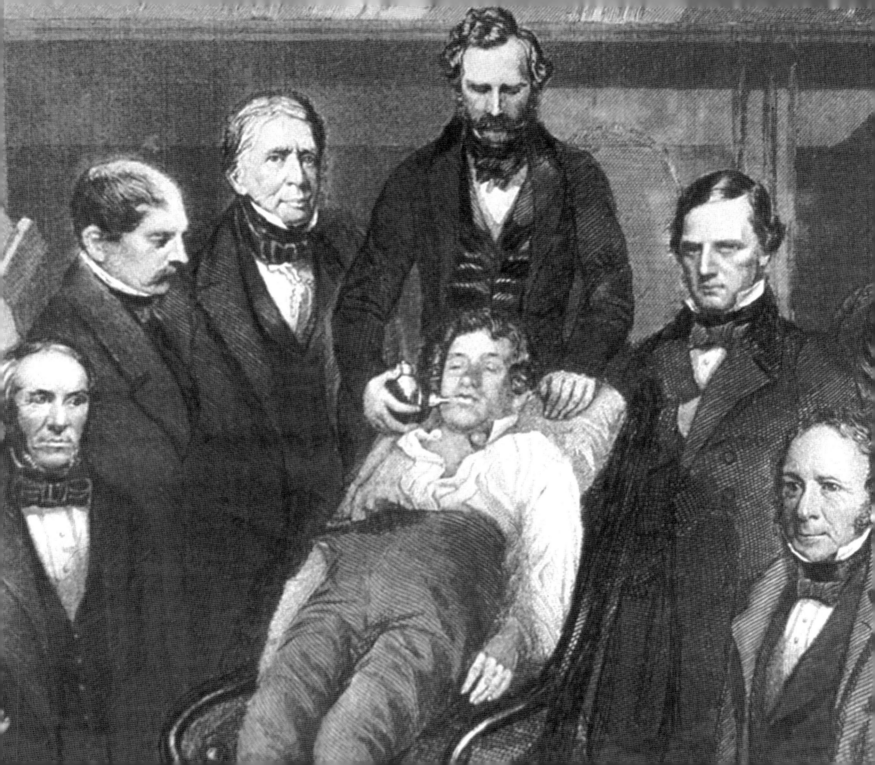

RUBBER GLOVES IN SURGERY

The first use of rubber gloves during a surgical procedure occurred not because of the patient or concerns about antiseptic conditions, but because of a nurse.

Caroline Hampton graduated from nursing school at New York Hospital in 1888. Johns Hopkins Hospital in Baltimore, Maryland, opened the following year, and surgeon William S. Halsted appointed her chief nurse of the operating room. Hampton's hands soon became irritated by the disinfectant chemicals mercuric chloride and carbolic acid. Halsted asked the Goodyear Rubber Company to make two pairs of thin rubber gloves Hampton could wear to protect her hands. The gloves were tested and worked so well the hospital ordered additional pairs. Within a few years, a medical publication suggested all members of surgical teams wear gloves.

Physicians on both sides were poorly trained and not prepared to treat disease. Many soldiers came from small towns and farms and had not been exposed to diseases such as measles, scarlet fever, diphtheria, and smallpox. The soldiers had no immunity against these deadly illnesses as they swept through entire regiments.

Despite terrible losses of men to illness and wounds, the war helped medicine move into the modern age through better recordkeeping. Doctors kept track of which treatments worked and which did not. Cleaner and brighter field hospitals replaced temporary medical facilities, later becoming models for hospitals throughout the United States. Contrary to popular belief, anesthesia was often available, and either chloroform or ether was given to patients. A new system of evaluating battlefield injuries was started, allowing the most serious cases to be treated first. Ambulances were sent out systematically, replacing the haphazard carting away of the wounded in wagons. Surgeons learned new techniques, such as how to stop blood loss quicker, that would become common practice after the war.

Elizabeth BLACKWELL

Born in 1821, Elizabeth Blackwell was first employed as a teacher, but she found herself increasingly interested in medicine—a field no woman had yet breeched. In 1847, the Geneva Medical School of Western New York accepted her as a student. According to legend, she got in because her application was thought to be a joke. After she graduated in 1849, no hospital in the United States or England would let her practice medicine. She bought a house to begin a private practice since no landlord would rent her space. As a public speaker Blackwell was a tireless champion of women's rights, especially in medicine. Even as she struggled to establish herself in medicine, the world's first woman's medical college, the Female Medical College of Pennsylvania, opened in Philadelphia in 1850.

SEEING INSIDE

X rays allow doctors to see inside their patients without surgery. They are indispensible to modern medicine. But the discovery of X rays took years and the cumulative efforts of several scientists who grasped pieces of the puzzle without putting everything together.

One of these scientists was Sir William Crookes. He was an English physicist who in 1861 discovered the element thallium. He also developed the Crookes tube, a glass tube with a partial vacuum that contains two electrodes. When high voltage electricity passes from one electrode to the other, it produces cathode rays, or streams of electrons. During experiments with the tube, Crookes would sometimes place unexposed photographic plates on the table he was using. When he tried to use the plates later, they had shadows on them. Not realizing the plates had been exposed to a new type of radiation, Crookes complained to the manufacturer it had sent him damaged plates.

X rays quickly became a powerful tool for doctors after their 1895 discovery.

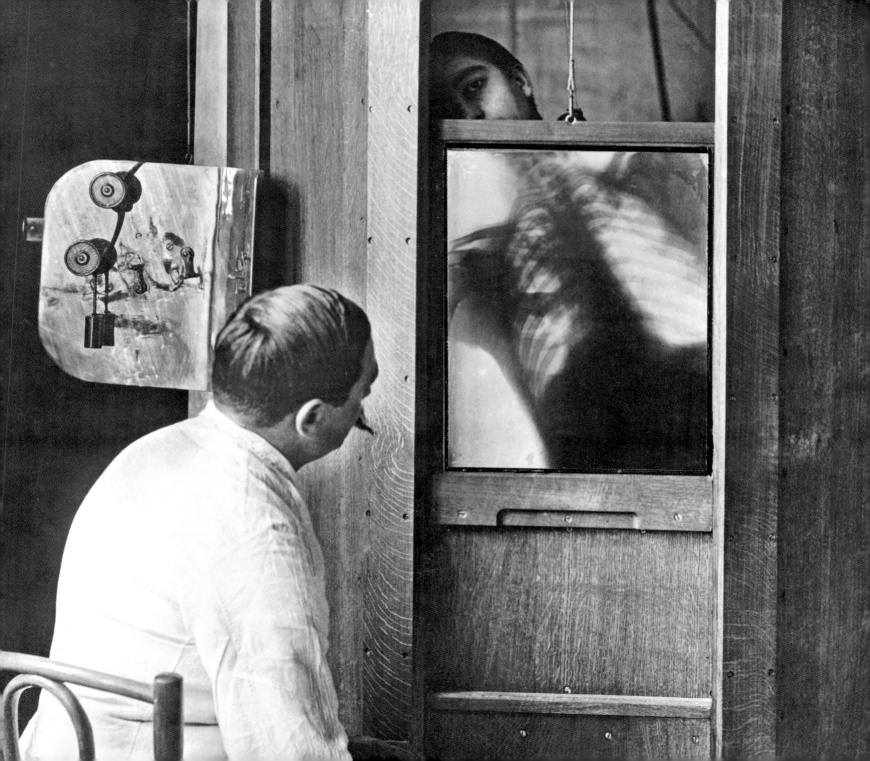

MEDICAL INSTRUMENT DISCOVERIES

Two of today's most commonplace medical instruments were invented near the end of the 1800s and the beginning of the 1900s. In 1896, Italian doctor Scipione Riva-Rocci devised a rubber bag that went around the arm and was filled with air to measure blood pressure. Nine years later, Russian Nikolai Korotkoff began placing a stethoscope at the pit of the elbow to listen for the sound the blood makes when the air from the cuff cuts off circulation, allowing a more accurate blood pressure reading.

In 1901, Dutch doctor Willem Einthoven attached a galvanometer (used to measure current) to a device that projected a record of its readings onto a photographic plate. This created an image of the heart wave. Every time the heart beats, a wave of electric current crosses the plate from right to left. This device was the forerunner to today's electrocardiogram test (EKG), which checks the heart's electric activity.

The Discovery of X Rays

German physicist Wilhelm Conrad Röntgen was born on March 27, 1845, in Lennep, Germany. He studied at the mechanical technical school in Zurich, Switzerland, developing a reputation for building complicated, intricate instruments. Beginning in 1876, he served as a professor of physics at a succession of German universities.

Röntgen began conducting research into the new field of cathode rays in the 1890s. On the afternoon of November 8, 1895, he was working alone in his laboratory. Covering a Crookes tube completely with black cardboard, he decided to test it to make sure no light escaped when he passed electric current through it. Röntgen darkened the room and shot current through the tube. Upon doing so, he was pleased because no light seemed to have slipped out. He was just about to stop the current when he noticed something out of the corner of his eye. A strange, shimmering glow seemed to be coming from a surface a little way away from the tube. The surface was coated with the chemical barium platinocyanide.

Röntgen studied electricity and the properties of crystals as well as X rays.

X RAYS IN COURT

It did not take long for the United States and Europe to accept X rays as evidence in legal matters. In December 1896, a US judge ruled X rays could be used as evidence in a case charging malpractice against a physician. The doctor had prescribed special exercises to a student who had fallen from a ladder to help heal his injured leg. The exercises caused the student tremendous pain. An X ray revealed a bone fracture. The fractured ends of the bone were not aligning correctly, probably because of the exercises. The student won the case.

At first Röntgen thought some light had escaped from the tube after all and was being reflected. But the same thing happened again when he repeated the test. He struck a match for illumination and was surprised to find the surface area itself was glowing. Röntgen guessed some new type of ray other than cathode rays must be coming from the Crookes tube, causing the screen to glow.

Röntgen began excitedly experimenting for hours on end, hardly eating or sleeping for weeks and barely seeing his wife. Finally, he invited her down to his laboratory to show her what he was doing. He placed her hand on an undeveloped photographic plate and sent current through a Crookes tube he had placed above her hand. He then developed the plate and showed it to her. Shockingly, they could see the bones of her hand, along with the solid dark outline of a ring she had on one finger.

The new ray Röntgen had discovered was the X ray, initially named because it was so mysterious. Röntgen knew exactly what type of excitement this news would create when it was made public. After mailing information about

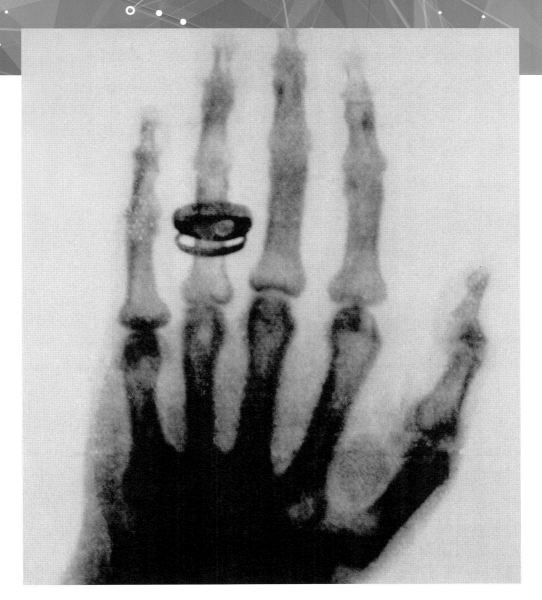

One of Röntgen's earliest surviving X ray images

the discovery to a professional journal and some colleagues, he turned to his wife and announced: "Now there will be the Devil to pay!"[1]

Indeed, the reaction was swift. Most people praised the discovery, realizing the incredible potential of something that allowed doctors to peer inside the body without cutting it open. A few criticized Röntgen for unleashing a mysterious power they believed would inevitably destroy humanity.

The medical establishment quickly embraced this new innovation. Just a few months later, in March 1896, physicians in Chicago, Illinois, in the United States were talking about how X rays had shown not only bones in the hand and leg but metal items in a pocketbook.

Other scientists immediately began experiments. In the lab of American inventor Thomas Edison, Clarence Madison Dally studied X rays and quickly worked up an X ray device called a fluoroscope. Dally died several years later of cancer caused by his enthusiastic X ray experiments.

THE DARK SIDE OF X RAYS

With all of their power for healing, X rays also have a hidden danger: radiation. At first X rays were treated like toys. X ray machines popped up in department stores, arcades, and shoe stores as a source of amusement. People happily took X ray pictures of their feet and watched the bones move as they wiggled their toes. But soon those who consistently exposed themselves to X rays began getting sick. Clarence Dally lost his hair, his left hand, and several more fingers to radiation poisoning, dying soon afterward.

The famous Polish scientist Marie Curie was another radiation casualty. She helped pioneer a mobile X ray unit for the French army in World War I, founded a radiological school for nurses, and won a Nobel Prize in Physics (1903) and Chemistry (1911). She died of leukemia as a result of prolonged exposure to radiation.

a   *b*

It was also in 1896 that Walter Bradford Cannon, an American physiologist, used a fluoroscope to follow the path of barium sulfate through an animal's digestive system. Some consider this to be the first medical use of X rays.

In 1901, Röntgen became the first winner of the Nobel Prize in Physics. Unwilling to profit from a discovery he knew would benefit all humanity, he donated his prize money to the University of Wurzburg.

Chickens and Frogs
ADVANCE MEDICINE

$$\frac{a+b}{a} = \frac{a}{b} = 1.618$$

S ometimes medical advancements come from unexpected places. A Dutch physician probably never realized his chickens would unlock the key to a medical mystery. And it was likewise unexpected when the researcher who was seeking to understand how nerves grow found a technique that would become vital in saving thousands of lives.

The Discovery of Vitamins

Typically affecting sailors who were at sea for long periods, doctors had been familiar with scurvy since the days of the ancient Greeks. Scurvy is a nutritional deficiency caused by a lack of vitamin C in a person's diet. Its symptoms include fatigue, damage to the gums, and loose teeth.

People guessed at cures for nutritional deficiencies such as scurvy long before they understood vitamins.

As sailing ships took to the seas in great numbers after the voyages of Christopher Columbus, it was impossible for ships to stay at sea for long without much of the crew getting scurvy. In 1536, while exploring Canada, one-quarter of French explorer Jacques Cartier's crew died of scurvy.[1] Many of the rest were near death. They were saved when a person from a local tribe showed them how to make a tea of pine needles. In 1593, English Admiral Sir Richard Hawkins reported that 10,000 men in his command had died from scurvy.[2] He also noted that giving them an orange or lemon every day stopped the disease. The British navy, however, ignored his recommendation.

In 1747, aboard the frigate *Salisbury*, English physician James Lind gave an orange a day to sailors who were near death, then watched them completely recover. He soon published a book about his experiences, *Treatise on the Scurvy*, but it failed to reach a wide audience. This direct evidence of a cure for scurvy did not fit the current theories of disease, making it difficult for the medical establishment to accept it. Fully understanding scurvy required a much better understanding of the role vitamins played in diet, which did not come until the 1900s.

Beriberi and Hungry Chickens

In 1882, natives in the Dutch East Indies (today Indonesia) rebelled against colonial rule. Dutch soldiers sent to fight the rebellion contracted a wasting disease called beriberi, which was uncommon before the Europeans came to the region. A team

William A. HINTON

As the 1900s progressed, some of the most feared diseases began succumbing to medical advancements. An African-American doctor helped diagnose one of these illnesses: syphilis. William A. Hinton was born on December 15, 1883, in Chicago, Illinois. Both of his parents were former slaves. A brilliant student, he finished the Harvard University medical program in three years instead of four. However, because he was African American, he was forbidden from treating patients at any of Boston's hospitals. He went to work for the Wassermann Laboratory at Harvard, focusing on syphilis research. In 1915, the Wassermann Laboratory was transferred to the Massachusetts Department of Public Health, and Hinton was appointed director. In 1927, he developed the Hinton test for diagnosing syphilis. Hinton's test became the accepted method worldwide for diagnosing syphilis. He later helped develop an improved test for syphilis diagnosis called the Davies-Hinton test.

of Dutch physicians, including Christiaan Eijkman, was sent to Java to look for the microbe that caused the disease. Although the other physicians thought they had found it, Eijkman suspected otherwise and kept working.

He kept some chickens that had also contracted beriberi. He fed them a diet of polished white rice. When Eijkman left town for a few days, a servant fed the chickens unpolished brown rice instead. The chickens completely recovered. When Eijkman returned to find the healthy chickens, he realized beriberi was not caused by a microbe but was instead related to diet.

Eijkman proposed what he called "essential food factors."[3] Although his report was met with a storm of criticism, subsequent research proved a substance in the husks of rice actually protected against beriberi. This same substance was removed when the rice was polished. Eijkman's findings eventually led to the medical acceptance of the idea that a healthy diet required specific elements.

In 1911, Polish biochemist Casimir Funk stated that this disease-stopping substance in foods belonged to a group of organic chemical compounds called amines, and invented the word *vitamine* for these "vital amines." It was later realized that not all of these compounds were amines, so the word was changed to *vitamin*. Funk said vitamins were important for good health and proposed that the lack of a particular vitamin can cause disease.

The discovery of vitamins has allowed doctors to cure many nutritional deficiencies, such as goiters, enlarged neck glands.

Today there are 13 officially recognized vitamins. Research about vitamins continues, including how they are obtained from certain foods and if the use of supplements can take the place of obtaining vitamins from diet.

Tissue Culture

Sometimes, as in the case of van Leeuwenhoek's discovery of tiny organisms in his microscope, the long-range medical potential of a discovery is not immediately apparent. Such was the case with the discovery of tissue culture.

Ross Granville Harrison was born on January 13, 1870, in Germantown, Pennsylvania. In the summer of 1890, he participated in a project about oyster embryology, which led to a lifelong interest in the study of embryos and development.

In 1906, Harrison began researching how nerves developed. He realized that to do this he would have to observe under his microscope tissues that contained nothing but nerve cells. If he could keep these cells alive and vital for a period of time, perhaps he could witness what developed.

"Because of tissue culture more has been learned about the basic mechanisms of disease in the past fifty years than in the previous five thousand."[4]

—*Physicians and authors Meyer Friedman and David Friedland*

He took nerves from the brain of a frog, placed them on a microscope slide in a solution of frog blood plasma, placed a cover on it, sealed it with

Today, Harrison's discovery of tissue culture allows doctors to grow skin and other organs.

wax to prevent evaporation, and began his observations. As he later wrote: "When reasonable aseptic precautions are taken, tissues live under these conditions for a week and in some cases, specimens have been kept alive for nearly four weeks."[5] As Harrison watched nerve fibers grow from the nerve cell, he was unaware he had developed tissue culture—the ability to grow living cells in a laboratory environment.

The Immortal Chicken Heart

A few years later, French physician Alexis Carrel realized the monumental importance of Harrison's discovery of tissue culture. His assistant, Montrose Burrows, discovered chicken plasma was better than frog plasma for growing tissue.

Carrel kept chicken heart tissue alive for 120 days in 1912 and received a lot of publicity. One of his assistants, Albert Eberling, then made a few changes to Carrel's methods and kept a microscopic piece of a chicken heart alive for more than three decades. If it got too big as it grew, Eberling would cut it in half and start both pieces growing again. He claimed he did this for 34 years. Because this one piece lived so long, newspapers called it the "immortal" chicken heart.

Tissue culture has made it possible to study living organisms at cellular and molecular levels. This has aided the study of diseases and the development of vaccines for illnesses such as measles and mumps. Tissue culture opened up a vast realm of possibilities for medical researchers.

Carrel was a noted surgeon who devised a new way to treat wounds during World War I.

The Discovery of Insulin

The discovery of insulin in 1921 by Canadians Frederick Banting and Charles Best was big news for diabetes sufferers. Diabetes comes from the Greek word for "sieve" because the disease causes excessive thirst and then frequent urination as the body discharges the liquid. Before the discovery of insulin, diabetes meant certain death.

Progress in understanding the disease was slow. In the 1700s, Englishman Matthew Dobson realized the sweetness in the urine of diabetes patients came from sugar. In 1889, two Germans, Oskar Minkowski and Joseph von Mering, confirmed the pancreas played a central role in diabetes. But except for a starvation diet that kept diabetics alive for a bit longer, there was no known treatment for the disease.

In 1921 at the University of Toronto, Banting and Best made an extract from pancreatic material. They tested it on dogs that had their pancreases removed. It worked. The extract functioned like the removed body part, regulating the animal's blood sugar levels. Banting and Best named the extract *isletin*, which was later changed to *insulin*.

In 1922, doctors at Toronto General Hospital gave an improved version of the extract to Leonard Thompson, a 14-year-old dying of diabetes. After he showed great improvement, the extract was given to other diabetic children, most of them comatose and dying. In one of medicine's most dramatic moments, the first children began waking up even before the last children received the extract.

In 2012, the American Diabetes Association estimated there were more than 29 million Americans with some form of diabetes.[6] Many have to take insulin.

Best, *left*, and Banting with the first dog kept alive by insulin

BEAUTIFUL MOLD

It is impossible to accurately say how many lives antibiotics have saved since the introduction of penicillin. The number is certainly in the millions. Because of that, it is no exaggeration to say antibiotics are some of the most important medical discoveries of the 1900s and all time.

John Tyndall was one of England's most famous doctors. One day in 1875, after conducting an experiment, he noticed a colorful mold had formed inside some of his test tubes of bacteria. Where the mold was thickest, the bacteria was dead. Tyndall observed this condition several years before it became common knowledge that bacteria caused disease. Thus, he limited his observations on this to a few sentences in a 47-page article, and a great opportunity to discover the first antibiotic was missed. It would be decades before another doctor would pick up where Tyndall's research left off.

That doctor, Alexander Fleming, was born in Scotland on August 6, 1881. On the battlefields of France in World War I (1914–1918), Fleming saw thousands of wounded

The accidental discovery of the antibiotic properties of the penicillin mold has saved countless lives.

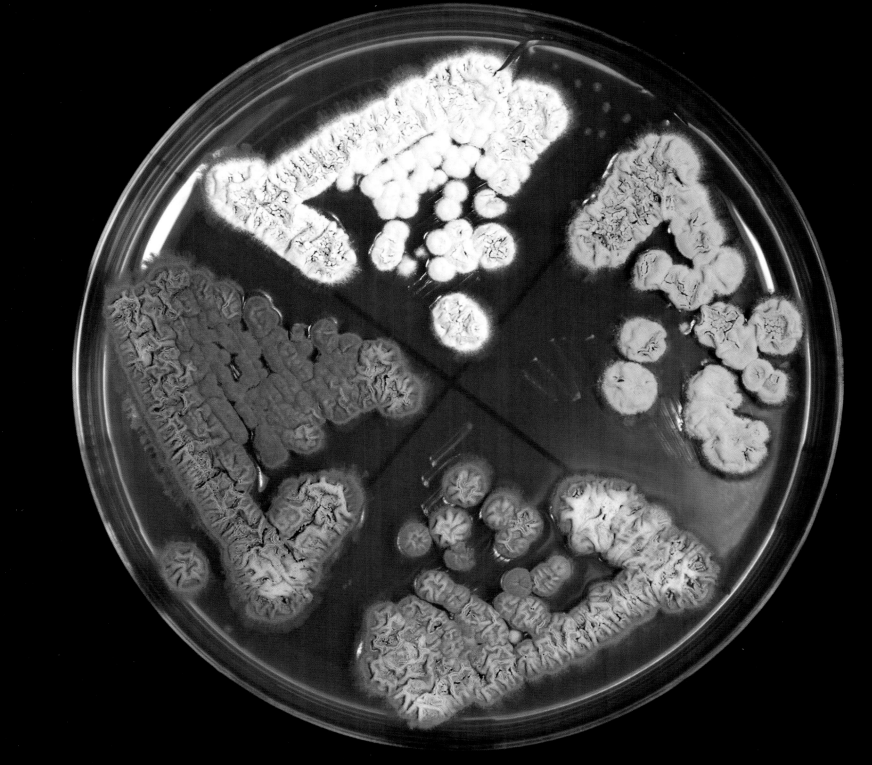

EARLY ANTIBIOTICS

Before penicillin there was Prontosil. Prontosil was discovered in the early 1930s at Germany's I.G. Farbenindustrie company and sold as a red dye. Gerhard Domagk, the director of the company's department of pathology and bacteriology, had it tested for other uses. Tests revealed it cured streptococcal infections in mice. Domagk published the results and Prontosil became a popular medicine. One of the first people treated with it was Domagk's daughter, who had contracted a streptococcal infection from a needle prick. Domagk was nominated for a Nobel Prize in 1939 for his discovery, but Germany's government under the Nazi Party would not let him accept it. Prontosil was later eclipsed by penicillin, a more powerful antibiotic.

soldiers, their injuries filled with dirt and pieces of metal. He knew their bodies' defense mechanisms would not be enough to destroy the germs and bacteria that were entering them. "Surrounded by all those infected wounds, by men who were suffering and dying without our being able to do anything to help them, I was consumed by a desire to discover, after all this struggling and waiting, something which would kill those microbes," he said.[1]

The Fortunate Vacation

In 1928, Fleming was preparing to go on a two-week vacation. On the floor below him, another researcher was growing the mold *Penicillium notatum*. Since the mold spores were very light, some of them got into the air and floated up the stairs to Fleming's laboratory. Thus when Fleming opened a petri dish to smear it with staphylococcus bacteria, the surrounding air was full of mold spores. Unbeknownst to Fleming, some of the spores settled on the small dish. Fleming closed the dish and placed it on his laboratory bench before leaving for vacation. Normally he would have placed the dish in his incubator to make the bacteria grow quickly. However, since he was leaving on vacation, he knew

Fleming's work increased scientific understanding of the immune system and the side effects of antibiotics on animals.

the bacteria would grow just fine under normal conditions at room temperature during the time he was away, so he left the dish out.

Upon his return from vacation, Fleming noticed the petri dish was full of mold, which was not unusual. What was unexpected was that the bacteria, normally yellow, were clear closest to the mold. Clear bacteria are no longer alive. But what had killed them? Fleming decided to investigate. He found the mold killed harmful bacteria even when diluted 600 times.[2] He had discovered penicillin, an antibiotic that kills certain types of bacteria.

The discovery of penicillin is considered one of medicine's most fortunate events. The mold spores were in the air and found the petri dish when Fleming opened it at precisely the right moment. If Fleming had not been going on vacation, he would have placed the petri dish containing the bacteria in his incubator, where the temperature, 100 degrees Fahrenheit (38°C), would have grown the bacteria but prevented the mold from growing. Likewise, if he had put another bacterial strain that was immune to penicillin on the petri dish, the mold would not have had any effect.

BLOOD BANKS SAVE MORE LIVES

Another important medical discovery that saved thousands of lives each year was made by African-American physician Charles R. Drew. Drew was drawn to the field of blood research as a medical student in the 1930s. At the time, blood spoiled quickly in storage. Drew had watched people die from loss of blood because donors couldn't be found in time. Drew discovered that by separating the plasma from the whole blood and then refrigerating each separately, they could be combined as long as a week later and be perfectly ready for use. This method became the model for setting up blood banks throughout the United States and Europe.

Everything fell perfectly into place for Fleming to make one of the most monumental medical discoveries of all time.

The importance of the discovery wasn't recognized right away. Fleming presented his findings in 1929, but few other scientists noticed. But by 1940, the thousands of casualties of World War II (1939–1945) made the search for an antibacterial agent urgent, and Fleming's 1929 paper was rediscovered. Three researchers at Oxford University in England, Howard Florey, Ernst Chain, and Norman Heatley, read Fleming's paper on penicillin, made some of the antibiotic, tested it, and found that it worked wonders. By June 1944, enough penicillin was being produced to treat all the injured Allied soldiers.[3]

The Discovery of Streptomycin

The success of penicillin set off a rush to discover other antibiotics. The first was streptomycin. In 1943 at Rutgers College in New Jersey, streptomycin was discovered from a microbe living freely in garden material on the Rutgers College farm. It was tested at the Mayo Clinic in Rochester,

ALZHEIMER'S DISEASE

Even as the 1900s brought new discoveries like penicillin to cure age-old ailments, it also saw new illnesses become pervasive, including Alzheimer's. In the autumn of 1906, German doctor Alois Alzheimer presented the case of "Frau Auguste D" to a group of scientists. The woman was in her early 50s and had been brought to him in 1901. Her symptoms included memory loss, difficulty in speaking and understanding, and suspicions that her husband was cheating on her. Her condition steadily worsened. She had died the previous spring.

Frustrated by his inability to treat her, Alzheimer performed an autopsy. He discovered the woman's brain had suffered severe shrinkage, particularly in the cortex. Alzheimer also found the woman's brain contained dead and dying brain cells as well as small blood vessels with extensive fatty deposits. Ultimately this condition was named after Alzheimer. Today it is the sixth-leading cause of death in the United States. There is still no cure.

Minnesota, and found to be effective in treating bacterial infections that had resisted penicillin.

Credit for this discovery ignited a controversy that continues to this day. Ukrainian-born Selman Waksman has usually been given credit for the discovery, and he won a Nobel Prize for it in 1952. However, a graduate student at Rutgers, Dr. Albert Schatz, also claimed credit for the discovery. The two fought a bitter legal battle over it. In 2010, material was discovered at Rutgers that seemed to bolster Schatz's discovery claims. The controversy remains unresolved.

Each antibiotic discovered has a limited period of usefulness. Bacteria evolve very quickly, and they soon become resistant to existing antibiotics. Misuse of antibiotics—for instance, taking antibiotics for colds caused by viruses—allows bacteria to develop defenses to these drugs. Thus the search for new antibiotics is continuous.

Waksman, *center*, and lab associates test streptomycin in their Rutgers University lab.

Medicine
MARCHES ON

Medicine's progress over the last century has been astounding. From the discovery of DNA to new surgical techniques using tiny computerized instruments to new treatments for diseases such as AIDS that once seemed unstoppable, medicine has moved forward at an amazing pace. There is still much to do—new treatments to discover, new diseases to combat, new surgical advancements to be made. Medicine never stands still. A look at even a few of medicine's most astounding achievements over the last 100 years is enough to underscore its vital importance to modern life.

$$\frac{a+b}{a} = \frac{a}{b} = 1.618$$

DNA research is only one of many paths for future medical advances.

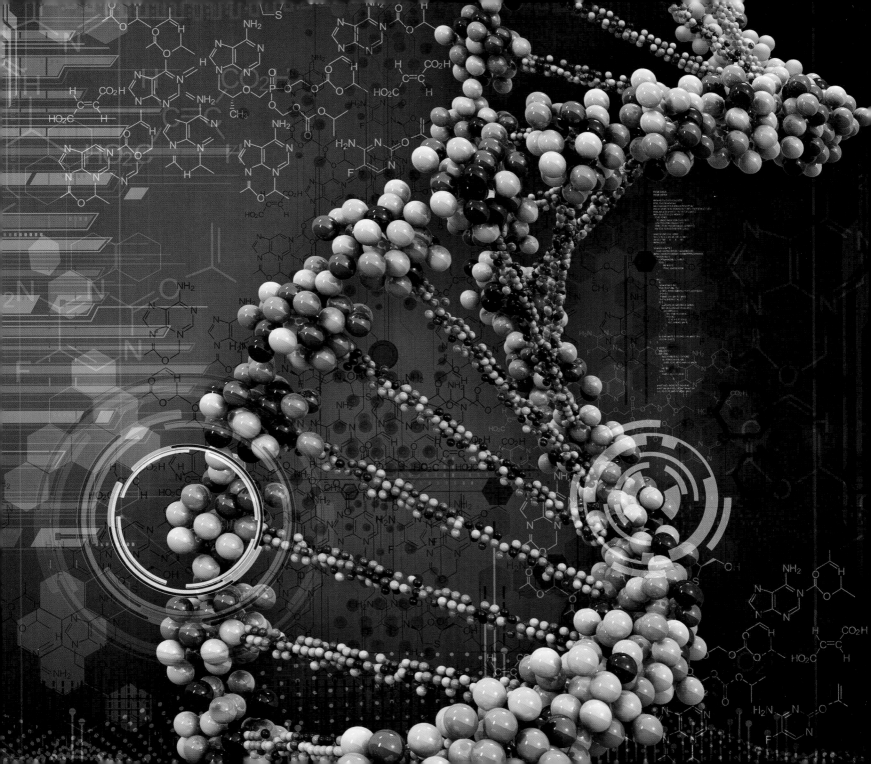

Discovering DNA

The discovery of deoxyribonucleic acid (DNA) is one of medicine's greatest triumphs of the last century. DNA research actually dates to the 1800s. In 1869, Johann Friedrich Miescher, a Swiss biochemist working in Germany, obtained pus-filled bandages from a hospital and isolated from them a substance he called nuclein. He discovered this nuclein was found only in chromosomes (which had been discovered in 1842 by Swiss botanist Karl Wilhelm von Nägeli) and realized it was a new type of organic molecule. He knew this had something to do with heredity, writing in 1893: "Inheritance insures a continuity in form from generation to generation."[1]

By 1944, building on prior research, American scientist Oswald Avery had shown DNA carries genetic information. In 1953, James Watson and Francis Crick illustrated what DNA looked like in the journal *Nature*. In 1962, Watson, Crick, and another

DNA'S OTHER DISCOVERER

Rosalind Franklin was born on July 25, 1920, in London, England. She earned her doctorate in physical chemistry from Cambridge University in 1945, after which she joined a research group and was charged with determining the structure of DNA. Franklin presented her findings in 1951 at a seminar attended by fellow DNA researcher James Watson. She had discovered the molecule can exist in two forms (which she called A and B) depending on the humidity in the air. She also specified how much water the molecule contained. These were crucial points that helped Crick and Watson publish their groundbreaking representation of the DNA molecule in 1953.

Franklin died in 1958 at the age of 37 from ovarian cancer. Because Nobel Prize rules forbade deceased people being nominated, she was not nominated for the Nobel Prize won in 1962 by Watson, Crick, and Wilkins. Many feel she and her work have been overlooked.

a

b

researcher, Maurice Wilkins, jointly received the Nobel Prize in Physiology or Medicine for their work on DNA.

The future for DNA research and application holds much promise. Diseases could be cured through the use of gene therapy, which would replace damaged genes with healthy ones. Doctors might even be able to predict the possibility of a person contracting a medical condition, such as heart disease, years in the future by examining their DNA. This would allow people to take steps to prevent problems years away.

David Ho Combats AIDS

When acquired immunodeficiency syndrome (AIDS) burst onto the scene in the early 1980s, medical researchers scrambled to find a way to fight it. David Ho discovered the answer. He was born in 1952 in Taiwan. He saw some of the first documented AIDS cases as a medical resident at UCLA Medical Center and decided to concentrate on fighting this new disease.

It often took months or years for people with human immunodeficiency virus (HIV), the virus that causes AIDS, to

AIDS: A MODERN PLAGUE

AIDS is a disease of the immune system caused by HIV. Although it is uncertain how AIDS originated, it is generally accepted that it began in Africa. By 1980, AIDS had spread to five continents: North America, South America, Europe, Africa, and Australia. In the United States, the first recognized cases of AIDS were in the early 1980s when a number of homosexual men in New York and California developed infections and cancers that were resistant to treatment. Soon HIV was discovered, and it ultimately became clear that HIV causes AIDS. HIV and AIDS are epidemic in parts of the world. In areas of Africa, more than one in five adults are infected with HIV.[2]

become seriously ill. Many doctors initially concluded the virus went dormant after it was contracted. Ho's research found just the opposite; the virus multiplied quickly from the very beginning, eventually exhausting the patient's immune system. Ho's discovery changed how researchers attacked the illness, moving their focus from its final months to the beginning stages. Ho developed mixtures of drugs for fighting the disease that provided real hope for thousands.

Since the epidemic began, 1,155,792 people in the United States have been diagnosed with AIDS. It is estimated 1.3 million people are living with HIV in the United States alone.[3] Tens of millions of people around the world are affected. As of 2014 there was no cure. But advanced drugs have already turned what was once an almost-certain death sentence into a long-term manageable condition.

Robotic Surgery

Surgery advanced by leaps and bounds in the 1900s. Knowledge of blood groups and transfusion techniques, the use of antibiotics, and an understanding of blood clotting and anticlotting methods have saved many lives. New surgical innovations, such as stapling instruments that can join blood vessels or tissues quicker and easier than hand sewing and the development of diagnostic tools such as computerized tomography (CT) scans and magnetic resonance imaging (MRI) gave surgeons advantages and opportunities not dreamed of 100 years before.

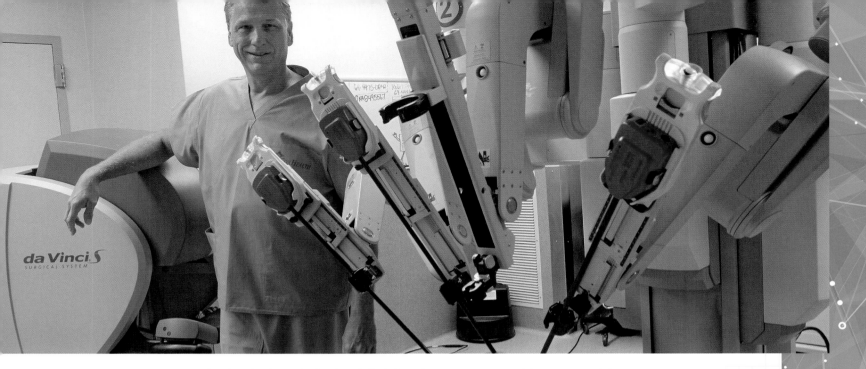

The Da Vinci surgical robot is helping doctors operate with more precision.

Surgery is still moving forward at lightning speed. With the increasing use of computers in medicine, robotic surgery is becoming more commonplace in the 2000s. Robotic surgery uses very small surgical tools attached to a robotic arm that a surgeon controls with a computer. Smaller, more precise movements are possible using this type of surgery. Procedures such as cutting away cancerous tissue from sensitive areas of the body, kidney transplants, and hip replacements can be performed by robotic surgery and voice-directed robotic surgery. Bionic limbs and artificial organ replacements offer exciting new horizons for research and life-saving improvements.

The First Heart Transplant

On December 3, 1967, newspaper headlines were filled with the extraordinary news that the world's first successful heart transplant had occurred in South Africa. Dr. Christiaan Barnard, a graduate of Cape Town medical school, performed the operation. The transplant occurred at Groote Schuur Hospital on 53-year-old Lithuanian Louis Washkansky, who had coronary heart disease and had suffered several heart attacks during the previous seven years.

Barnard used a technique initially developed in the United States in the 1950s. American Norman Shumway had performed the first successful heart transplant on a dog in 1958. The heart Barnard used was from 25-year-old Denise Darvall, who had been pronounced brain dead after a car accident. The operation was a success, and Washkansky lived for 18 days afterward. Unfortunately, the drugs he was given to stop his body from rejecting the new heart made him susceptible to disease, and he died of pneumonia. However, a new frontier in medicine had opened; a second heart transplant patient who underwent surgery in January 1968 lived 18 months.[4]

Initially, the difficulties in keeping the body from rejecting the new organ made some doctors and patients turn away from heart transplants. Today, sometimes medication can help solve this problem. Using an artificial heart can prolong life, although this is not a long-term solution. Researchers are developing ways to grow new organs using a patient's own tissue to solve the problem of rejection.

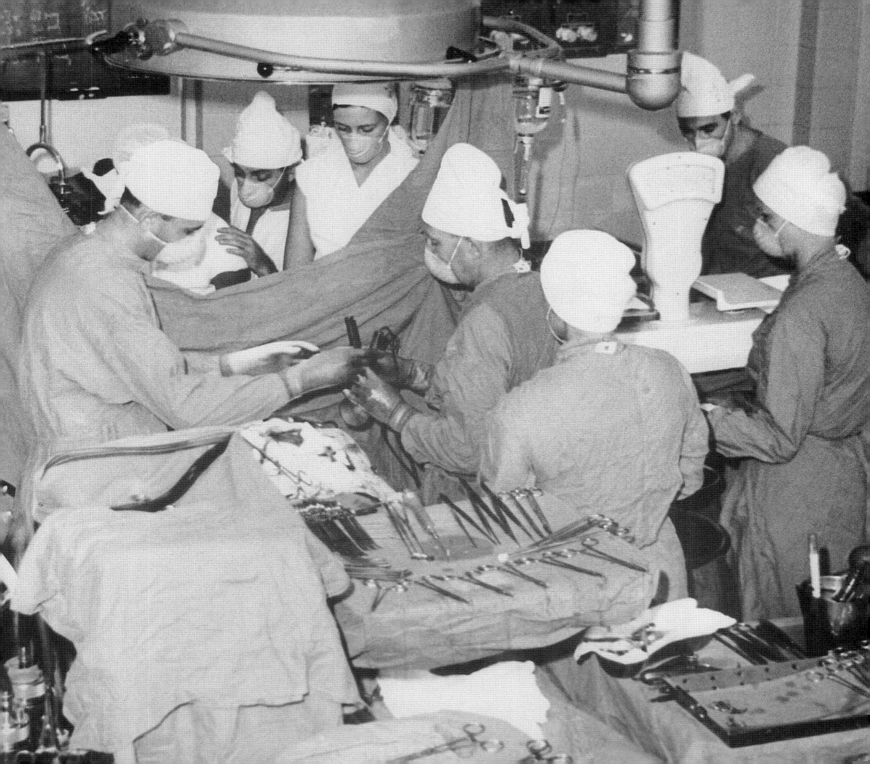

Medicine's Next Great Hero

Curing cancer. Preventing heart disease. Creating immunizations and better treatments for AIDS, avian flu, and Ebola. These are just some of the challenges facing the medical community today. There has been a tremendous amount of progress in medicine and the medical field over the centuries. Much has been accomplished. Much, however, remains to be done.

No one knows who the next great medical hero will turn out to be. Louis Pasteur wanted to be a chemist, yet he became one of medicine's towering figures, a man

EBOLA

Ebola—in full, the Ebola virus disease—is a deadly disease caused by a virus. It is named after the Ebola River in central Africa where the disease originated in humans. Ebola causes high fever, rash, and bleeding and is fatal in 50 to 90 percent of human cases.

The first outbreak of Ebola in 1976 killed more than 400 people in central Africa. In 1995, another outbreak in the Congo killed 250. In late 2013, an outbreak began in West Africa. Ebola spread quickly and soon infected thousands.

Ebola can only be spread through contact with the bodily fluids of an infected person. Recently dead bodies are particularly contagious. In West Africa, traditional burial practices involve touching the body of the deceased, which contributes to Ebola's spread.

To prevent the spread of the disease, officials in health and aid organizations educate local communities about the disease and how it spreads. They also isolate people who come in contact with the infected.

But despite the efforts of health workers and governments, Ebola was not contained to West Africa. The first US case of Ebola was reported in Dallas, Texas, in September 2014. The infected man had been in contact with an infected person in Liberia before traveling to the United States. The patient died in Dallas on October 8, 2014. The 2014 disaster was the worst outbreak of Ebola to date, with thousands killed.

a   b whose discoveries saved millions. Anton van Leeuwenhoek was a merchant when he discovered bacteria. Wilhelm Conrad Röntgen discovered X rays by accident. Elizabeth Blackwell never realized women would one day outnumber men in medical schools.

Medicine has certainly come a long way from the days when a physician who wanted to learn more about human anatomy had to steal corpses and keep them in his room. As technology advances, it will continue opening new horizons for medicine. Yet no matter how advanced things become, medicine will remain at its core, as it always has been, a matter of life and death.

> *"We look for medicine to be an orderly field of knowledge and procedure. But it is not. It is an imperfect science, an enterprise of constantly changing knowledge, uncertain information, fallible individuals, and at the same time lives on the line. There is science in what we do, yes, but also habit, intuition, and sometimes plain old guessing. The gap between what we know and what we aim for persists. And this gap complicates everything we do."*[5]
>
> —*Atul Gawande, surgeon, in* Complications: A Surgeon's Notes on an Imperfect Science

Timeline

460 BCE Greek doctor Hippocrates is born.

130 CE Galen, the leading voice of medicine for the next 1,000 years, is born in Pergamum.

800s One of the first European medical schools is founded in Salerno, Italy.

1170 Rogerius Salernitanus writes the first widely used surgical textbook in Europe.

1543 Andreas Vesalius publishes his book on human anatomy.

1628 William Harvey publishes his observation of blood circulation, revolutionizing medical thought.

1670s Antonie van Leeuwenhoek sees microorganisms through his microscope.

1717 Lady Montagu brings the practice of variolation to England.

1747 Englishman James Lind cures scurvy with citrus fruit.

1790s Edward Jenner works out a method for vaccinating people against smallpox using cowpox.

1842 Georgia surgeon Crawford Long uses ether as an anesthetic.

1849 Elizabeth Blackwell becomes the first female doctor in the United States.

1854 Louis Pasteur develops a process for destroying microorganisms using heat, now called pasteurization; John Snow ends a cholera outbreak in London, England, by proving how the disease spread through the community.

1865 Joseph Lister begins using an antisepsis process during surgery, slashing mortality rates.

1882 Christiaan Eijkman discovers the link between diet and beriberi, a nutritional deficiency.

1895 Wilhelm Röntgen discovers X rays.

1901 Nurse Clara Maass dies in yellow fever experiments.

1906 Ross Granville Harrison develops a process for making tissue cultures.

1911 Casimir Funk invents the term *vitamine*.

1927 William A. Hinton develops a test to diagnose syphilis.

1928 Alexander Fleming discovers penicillin.

1953 The structure of DNA is revealed.

1967 Christiaan Barnard performs the first successful heart transplant.

1980s The HIV/AIDS epidemic begins.

2000s Robotic surgery becomes more prevalent.

Essential Facts

KEY TECHNOLOGIES

Microscope

The development of the microscope in the 1670s paved the way for an understanding of germ theory, the foundation of modern medicine.

Anesthesia

The development of anesthesia in the 1840s allowed for longer and more invasive surgeries.

X rays

The discovery of X rays in 1895 allowed doctors to see inside patients' bodies without surgery.

Antibiotics

Beginning with penicillin, discovered in 1928, antibiotics have saved untold lives.

IMPACT ON SCIENCE

Each medical discovery allows doctors to save more lives. Many medical discoveries have a wider application in other fields of science, including the microscope, X rays, tissue culture, and DNA. Germ theory, anesthetics, and improved surgical techniques provided a foundation for today's medical practices and opened new avenues for discovery researchers are continuing to investigate.

KEY FIGURES IN MEDICINE

Galen dominated medical thought from his lifetime, in the 100s CE, through the Middle Ages.

Scientists of the Renaissance and early modern times including Andreas Vesalius and William Harvey used their powers of observation to overturn old ideas.

Experimentation during the 1700s and 1800s led Edward Jenner, Louis Pasteur, Joseph Lister, and others to refine medical understanding of disease and infection.

Christiaan Barnard ushered in modern surgery with the first successful heart transplant in 1967.

QUOTE

"We look for medicine to be an orderly field of knowledge and procedure. But it is not. It is an imperfect science, an enterprise of constantly changing knowledge, uncertain information, fallible individuals, and at the same time lives on the line. There is science in what we do, yes, but also habit, intuition, and sometimes plain old guessing. The gap between what we know and what we aim for persists. And this gap complicates everything we do."

—*Atul Gawande, surgeon, in* Complications: A Surgeon's Notes on an Imperfect Science

Glossary

aneurysm

A bulge in the wall of a blood vessel.

antiseptic

Having the property of killing microorganisms.

aseptic

Lacking bacteria or other microorganisms.

astrology

A system of divination that predicts the future based on the movement of the stars and planets.

beriberi

A disease caused by nutritional deficiencies including symptoms of inflammation and degeneration of the nerves, heart, and digestive system.

cauterize

To burn with a hot iron, typically to close a wound.

cortex

The layer of the brain vital to memory, thinking, judgment, and speech.

dissect

To cut apart to examine the structure.

embryology

The study of the formation and early development of living organisms.

enzyme

A protein that allows chemical reactions to occur in living organisms.

miasma

A poisonous gas given off by stagnant water and rotting piles of animal and vegetable matter.

microbe

A microorganism.

ophthalmology

The study of the structure and diseases of the eye.

physiology

The study of the functions and systems of living things.

plasma

The watery part of blood in which white and red blood cells are suspended.

privy

An outdoor bathroom with no plumbing.

secular

Not connected to religion.

smallpox

A viral disease characterized by fever and rash that often leads to death.

syphilis

A sexually transmitted bacterial disease that causes sores and rashes and if untreated can result in blindness, deafness, paralysis, or death.

Additional Resources

Selected Bibliography

Adler, Robert E. *Medical Firsts*. Hoboken, NJ: Wiley, 2004. Print.

Belofsky, Nathan. *Strange Medicine*. New York: Perigee, 2013. Print.

Further Readings

Hardman, Lizabeth. *History of Medicine*. Detroit, MI: Lucent, 2012. Print.

Sullivan, Otha Richard. *Black Stars: African-American Women Scientists and Inventors*. Hoboken, NJ: Wiley, 2009. Print.

Zuchora-Walske, Christine. *Antibiotics*. Minneapolis, MN: Abdo, 2014. Print.

Websites

To learn more about History of Science, visit **booklinks.abdopublishing.com**. These links are routinely monitored and updated to provide the most current information available.

For More Information

Mütter Museum of the College of Physicians of Philadelphia
19 South Twenty-Second Street
Philadelphia, PA 19103
215-563-3737

http://muttermuseum.org
The Mütter Museum features exhibits on the history of anatomy and medicine, including medical instruments and specimens of human anatomy.

National Museum of Health and Medicine
2500 Linden Lane
Silver Spring, MD 20910
301-319-3300

http://www.medicalmuseum.mil
Established during the Civil War, the National Museum of Heath and Medicine houses exhibits and collections related to the history of American medical practice, with a focus on research issues and military medicine.

Source Notes

Chapter 1. Life and Death

1. John Duffy. *The Healers*. New York: McGraw-Hill, 1976. Print. 196.

2. Otto L. Bettmann, PhD. *A Pictorial History of Medicine*. Springfield, IL: Charles C. Thomas, 1956. Print. 284.

3. Russell Roberts. *Discover the Hidden New Jersey*. New Brunswick, NJ: Rutgers UP, 1995. Print. 53.

4. John T. Cunningham. *The New Jersey Sampler*. Upper Montclair, NJ: New Jersey Almanac, 1964. Print. 14.

5. Nathan Belofsky. *Strange Medicine*. New York: Perigee, 2013. Print. 5.

6. Albert S. Lyons. "Medical History—Women in Medicine." *Health Guidance*. Health Guidance, 2014. Web. 16 Sept. 2014.

7. Otto L. Bettmann, PhD. *A Pictorial History of Medicine*. Springfield, IL: Charles C. Thomas, 1956. Print. 277.

Chapter 2. Medicine Begins

1. Roy Porter, ed. *Medicine: A History of Healing*. New York: Marlowe, 1997. Print. 21.

2. Robert Zoller. "Medieval and Renaissance Astrology and Medicine." *New Library*. Robert Zoller, 2000. Web. 16 Sept. 2014.

3. Roy Porter, ed. *The Cambridge Illustrated History of Medicine*. Cambridge, UK: Cambridge UP, 1996. Print. 79.

4. Ibid.

5. Otto L. Bettmann, PhD. *A Pictorial History of Medicine*. Springfield, IL: Charles C. Thomas, 1956. Print. 91.

6. Ibid. 92.

7. Ibid. 113.

8. Roy Porter, ed. *Medicine: A History of Healing*. New York: Marlowe, 1997. Print. 129.

Chapter 3. The Power of Observation

1. Robert E. Adler. *Medical Firsts*. Hoboken, NJ: Wiley, 2004. Print. 69.

2. Roy Porter, ed. *The Cambridge Illustrated History of Medicine*. Cambridge, UK: Cambridge UP, 1996. Print. 159.

3. Meyer Friedman, MD, and Gerald W. Friedland, MD. *Medicine's 10 Greatest Discoveries*. New Haven, CT: Yale UP, 1998. Print. 31.

4. Otto L. Bettmann, PhD. *A Pictorial History of Medicine*. Springfield, IL: Charles C. Thomas, 1956. Print. 211.

5. Roy Porter, ed. *Medicine: A History of Healing*. New York: Marlowe, 1997. Print. 132.

6. Meyer Friedman, MD, and Gerald W. Friedland, MD. *Medicine's 10 Greatest Discoveries*. New Haven, CT: Yale UP, 1998. Print. 41.

Chapter 4. Fighting Illness

1. Peter Radetsky. *The Invisible Invaders*. Boston: Little, 1991. Print. 16.

2. Meyer Friedman, MD, and Gerald W. Friedland, MD. *Medicine's 10 Greatest Discoveries*. New Haven, CT: Yale UP, 1998. Print. 66.

3. Ibid. 68.

4. Ibid. 69.

5. Philip Ranlet. "The British, the Indians, and Smallpox: What Actually Happened at Fort Pitt in 1763?" *Pennsylvania History* 67.3 (Summer 2000): n.pag. Web. 16 Sept. 2014.

6. Peter Radetsky. *The Invisible Invaders*. Boston: Little, 1991. Print. 26.

7. John Duffy. *The Healers*. New York: McGraw-Hill, 1976. Print. 29.

Source Notes Continued

8. "The Death of George Washington." *George Washington's Mount Vernon.* Mount Vernon Ladies' Association, 2014. Web. 16 Sept. 2014.

9. Howard W. Haggard. *From Medicine Man to Doctor.* Mineola, NY: Dover, 2004. Print. 360.

10. Wayne Martin. *Medical Heroes and Heretics.* Old Greenwich, CT: Devin-Adair, 1977. Print. 28.

11. "Joseph Lister and Antiseptic Surgery." *ABPI.* Association of the British Pharmaceutical Industry, 2014. Web. 16 Sept. 2014.

12. "Obstetrics and Midwifery." *Encyclopedia of Children and Childhood in History and Society.* Gale, 2008. Web. 16 Sept. 2014.

13. Roy Porter, ed. *Medicine: A History of Healing.* New York: Marlowe, 1997. Print. 38.

14. Nicholas L. Tilney. *Invasion of the Body.* Cambridge, MA: Harvard UP, 2011. Print. 72.

15. "Lister's Carbolic Spray." *Center for the History of Medicine.* Francis A. Countway Library, Harvard Medical School, n.d. Web. 16 Sept. 2014.

Chapter 5. Relieving Pain

1. Robert E. Adler. *Medical Firsts.* Hoboken, NJ: Wiley, 2004. Print. 83.

2. Ibid.

3. Nathan Belofsky. *Strange Medicine.* New York: Perigee, 2013. Print. 103.

4. Roy Porter, ed. *The Cambridge Illustrated History of Medicine.* Cambridge, UK: Cambridge UP, 1996. Print. 228.

5. Daniel J. Kim. "Triumph Over Pain: The Curiously Contentious History of Ether." *University of Ontario Medical Journal* 78.1 (2008): 93. Web. 16 Sept. 2014.

6. John Duffy. *The Healers.* New York: McGraw-Hill, 1976. 207.

7. Otto L. Bettmann, PhD. *A Pictorial History of Medicine.* Springfield, IL: Charles C. Thomas, 1956. Print. 270.

Chapter 6. Seeing Inside

1. Guy Williams. *The Age of Miracles*. Chicago: Academy Chicago, 1987. Print. 204.

Chapter 7. Chickens and Frogs Advance Medicine

1. Wayne Martin. *Medical Heroes and Heretics*. Old Greenwich, CT: Devin-Adair, 1977. Print. 49.

2. Ibid. 50.

3. Roy Porter, ed. *The Cambridge Illustrated History of Medicine*. Cambridge, UK: Cambridge UP, 1996. Print. 192.

4. Meyer Friedman, MD, and Gerald W. Friedland, MD. *Medicine's 10 Greatest Discoveries*. New Haven, CT: Yale UP, 1998. Print. 134.

5. Ibid. 137.

6. "Statistics about Diabetes." *American Diabetes Association*. American Diabetes Association, 2014. Web. 16 Sept. 2014.

Chapter 8. Beautiful Mold

1. Robert E. Adler. *Medical Firsts*. Hoboken, NJ: Wiley, 2004. Print. 142.

2. Ibid. 143.

3. Ibid. 145.

Chapter 9. Medicine Marches On

1. James D. Watson. *DNA: The Secret of Life*. New York: Knopf, 2003. Print. 36.

2. "Global HIV and AIDS Epidemic." *AVERT*. AVERT, 2014. Web. 16 Sept. 2014.

3. "US HIV and AIDS Statistics." *AVERT*. AVERT, 2014. Web. 16 Sept. 2014.

4. Roy Porter, ed. *The Cambridge Illustrated History of Medicine*. Cambridge, UK: Cambridge UP, 1996. Print. 239.

5. Atul Gawande. *Complications: A Surgeon's Notes on an Imperfect Science*. New York: Picador, 2002. Print. 7.

Index

Alzheimer's disease, 85
American Civil War, 56, 58
anatomy, 13, 16, 24, 27, 30, 97
ancient medicine, 11, 13, 14, 16, 18, 25,
    28, 30, 32, 38, 68
anesthesia, 50, 52, 53, 54–56, 58
antibiotics, 80, 82, 84–85, 87, 92
antisepsis, 47, 48, 49, 58
Aristotle, 30
astrology, 19
Avery, Oswald, 90

Babylon, 11, 14
Bacon, Roger, 21
bacteria, 37, 45, 46, 48, 80, 82, 84–85,
    87, 97
Banting, Frederick, 78
Barnard, Christiaan, 94
Barton, William, 53
beriberi, 70, 72
Best, Charles, 78
Black Death, 21–23
Blackwell, Elizabeth, 14, 59, 97
blood banks, 84
blood-letting, 19, 23
Burrows, Montrose, 76

Cannon, Walter Bradford, 67
carbolic acid, 48–49, 58
Carrel, Alexis, 76
Cesalpino, Andreas, 30
Charles V, 27
childbirth, 14, 48, 52
circulation, 30, 31–32, 34, 62
Colombo, Realdo, 30
colonial medicine, 41
Colton, Gardner, 54–55
cowpox, 41–43
Crick, Francis, 90–91
Crookes, William, 60, 62, 64
Curie, Marie, 66

Dally, Clarence Madison, 66
Davy, Humphrey, 53
de Chauliac, Guy, 22–23
Dioscorides, 52
disease, theories of, 18, 25, 37, 43, 45,
    46, 70, 71, 72, 76, 80, 91
dissection, 16, 24, 30, 32
DNA, 90–91
Dobson, Matthew, 78
Domagk, Gerhard, 82
Drew, Charles R., 84

Eberling, Albert, 76
Ebola, 96
Eijkman, Christiaan, 72
Einthoven, Willem, 62
epidemic, 8, 21–22, 40, 91–92

Fleming, Alexander, 80, 82, 84–85
Franklin, Rosalind, 90
Funk, Casimir, 72

Galen, 16, 18, 24, 25, 26–27, 28, 30
germs, 37, 40, 43, 45, 47–48, 82
Gorgas, William, 8, 11

Hampton, Caroline, 58
Harrison, Ross Granville, 74, 76
Harvey, William, 30–32, 34
Hawkins, Richard, 70
Hinton, William A., 71
Hippocrates, 16, 18
HIV/AIDS, 88, 91–92, 96
Ho, David, 91–92
humors, 16
Hunter, John, 34

infection, theories of, 46, 47–48,
    82, 87
inoculation, 38, 42–43
instruments, 34, 47, 48, 56, 62, 88, 92
insulin, 78
Islamic medicine, 30

Jackson, Charles T., 55–56
Jenner, Edward, 41–43
Jensen, Hans, 35

Koch, Robert, 46
Korotkoff, Nikolai, 62

laughing gas. *See* nitrous oxide
Lind, James, 70
Lister, Joseph, 47–49
Liston, Robert, 50, 52
Long, Crawford, 54
Lullius, Raymundus, 53

Maass, Clara, 6, 8, 10–11
medical schools, 14, 23, 31, 49, 55
Mering, Joseph von, 78
microbes, 43, 45, 46, 72, 82, 85
microscope, 35, 37, 43, 74
Middle Ages, 18, 19, 23, 30, 52
Miescher, Johann Friedrich, 90
military medicine, 27, 50, 56, 58, 80, 82, 85
Minkowski, Oskar, 78
Morton, William, 55–56

Nafis, Ibn an-, 30
nitrous oxide, 53–55

Padua, 24, 27, 31
Paracelsus, 25
Paré, Ambroise, 27
Pasteur, Louis, 43, 45, 46, 47, 48, 49, 96
penicillin, 80, 82, 84–85, 87
plague, 19, 21, 22, 23, 91
Plenciz, Marc von, 37
Priestly, Joseph, 53
Prontosil, 82
public health, 23, 47

radiation, 60, 66
Riva-Rocci, Scipione, 62
robotics, 92–93
Röntgen, Wilhelm Conrad, 62, 64, 66–67, 97
rubber gloves, 58

Salernitanus, Rogerius, 23–24
Santorio, Santorio, 34
Schatz, Albert, 87
scurvy, 68, 70
Semmelweis, Ignaz Philipp, 48
Servetus, Michael, 30
smallpox, 38, 40–43, 58
streptomycin, 85, 87
surgery, 11, 19, 34, 47–49, 50, 52, 54, 56, 58, 60, 92, 93, 94
syphilis, 71

tissue culture, 74, 76
transplants, 93, 94
Tyndall, John, 80

vaccination, 41–43, 76
van Leeuwenhoek, Antonie, 35, 37, 74, 97
Vesalius, Andreas, 24, 26–27, 30
vitamins, 68, 70, 72, 74

Waksman, Selman, 87
Warren, John Collins, 55–56
Washington, George, 41
Watson, James, 90–91
Wells, Horace, 54–56
Wilkins, Maurice, 90–91
women in medicine, 14, 59
World War II, 85
Wortley Montagu, Mary, 40

X rays, 60, 62, 64, 66–67, 97

yellow fever, 6, 8, 10–11

About the Author

Russell Roberts is an award-winning full-time freelance writer who has published more than 60 books for both children and adults, including the regional best sellers *Down the Jersey Shore* and *10 Days to A Sharper Memory*. Among his more than 50 children's books are examinations of the lives of Thomas Jefferson, Alexander Hamilton, Robert Goddard, Philo T. Farnsworth, Alicia Keys, Galileo, and Nostradamus, as well as a series about characters from Greek mythology, and volumes about the Statue of Liberty, Lincoln and the abolition of slavery, and life in ancient China.